Favorites

Garret Mathews

Design by Colin Mathews
www.newspaperwriter.com

"Garret Mathews understands the hunger readers have for true reality shows – not the faked-up junk on TV, but the stories of real people who live real lives in real places. And he tells those stories with a deft hand. He clearly knows that words carry the freight that can change our own lives and change the way we look at the lives of others."

Bill Tammeus is a former Kansas City Star columnist and past president of the National Society of Newspaper Columnists.

"This book of collected columns is a treasure."

Furman Bisher is a longtime columnist on the Atlanta Journal Constitution.

"A series of encounters with extraordinary ordinary people, great souls at the edges of our lives – Birdie Lee, a 91-year-old bootlegger who laughs at the courts; the 81-year-old veteran of three wars who still suffers with nightmares; the father trying desperately not to cry at his son's wedding as the couple thanks him with roses. Tales of the heart told with observant wit, humor, courage and the shock of insight…An adventure of the heart."

David Birney is a veteran actor

All columns originally published by:
The Evansville Courier & Press
300 East Walnut Street
Evansville, Ind. 47702

$14.95
ISBN 978-0-615-32474-6
51495>

INTRODUCTION

I started in the newspaper business in early 1972 at the Bluefield, W. Va., Daily Telegraph, 90 miles and a few mountain ranges from my native Abingdon, Va.

At one time or another, I was feature writer, news editor and sports editor. I wrote a weekly column until 1984 when it expanded to five days a week and became my main job. I compiled two books of columns that I called "Folks" and "Folks 2."

In 1987, I was hired to be the metro columnist for The Evansville, Ind., Courier (later, The Evansville Courier & Press), truly a life-changing event. This is my first book of columns since moving to the Midwest.

If nothing else, I'm relentless. Altogether, I've written more than 6,400 columns on everything from mail-order brides to Appalachian snake-handlers. I never missed a deadline. I loved it.

Unfortunately, I'm not doing the column any more. The past few years have been rough on the newspaper industry. We've lost advertisers. We've lost readers. Folks have more options with their free time. The Internet. Cable TV. Playing around with their cell phones.

The future for print is dim. Some corporate newspaper owners have filed bankruptcy. To save money, most have reduced the space devoted to news. To save paper, most have reduced the size of the product. In time, a morning edition won't weigh much more than a good-sized cobweb. I try not to think about it.

We don't have as many people in the newsroom. I've been reassigned from columns to metro and features. I dabble in sports.

So why did I do this book? It took weeks to select 80-some favorites from more than two decades of writing. It took months to get them properly edited and ready for the printer.

I guess not wanting to be forgotten is the biggest reason. When my grandchildren come along, I want them to know what their

Paw-Paw did for a living.

But there's a larger purpose.

This kind of column was once common in medium-sized newspapers all across the country. Its author made you laugh, stirred your emotions and introduced you to an assortment of characters you may not have met any other way.

We were writers who put our personalities on the pages of the newspaper. Readers knew from what we wrote the previous month and the previous year to anticipate what we might come up with next.

My circumstances aren't unique. The ranks of full-time columnists on metro and feature sections are thinning. Soon, I fear, the genre will exist only in yellowed clippings.

So this book of columns is my way of climbing to the highest building, opening the window and hollering out, "Once upon a time, I did this thing for a living and I'm very proud of it."

At my newspaper, the tradition of having a metro columnist dated to the 1950s. At other dailies, it goes back longer than that. At the risk of sounding too self-important, I think the absence of these voices is a slash in the fabric of Americana.

I've always believed that the quirky and down-and-out are much more interesting than those who hang out in penthouses. Readers turning to my space in the newspaper wouldn't be surprised to read about an exotic dancer who wants to be a herpetologist, or the 91-year-old woman who got caught yet again for bootlegging beer and whiskey, or a pauper who died and the only persons to show up (besides me) were the two men from the funeral home.

Rare was my column that had its origin in a press release. I took home stacks of newspapers from southwest Indiana, Western Kentucky and Southern Illinois, looking for something that would work for my next installment. I cultivated a small group of sources from outlying areas who knew what I liked to write about and called or e-mailed suggestions.

But countless times I left the office with no inkling of what would transpire. In a business that is becoming about as spontaneous as a space launch, it was nice to just wing it. I nosed around rural post offices, country stores and farm co-ops in search of the colorful and offbeat. And if there was an old man with a flowing white beard riding a mule down a dirt road with groceries in his saddlebags, well, he was mine.

I'm not interested in predicting who's going to win the election, and why didn't the council adopt the Westside sewer plan, and should more riverboat money be used to improve the city's infrastructure? I'd rather talk with a demolition derby driver, or an oldtimer who hand-loaded coal, or a fellow of modest means who gave $2,000 to the government to pay on the national debt because he believed it was the patriotic thing to do.

I like to write goof pieces about throwing my 16-pound shot put in the back yard, and finding out how far I can walk while carrying a 25-pound weight, and organizing an Over-40 baseball team that played against Pony League all-stars. Because it was my idea, I got to pitch. And, hey, I hit over .350.

Beginning of rant.

Some believe newspaper columnists can be replaced by Internet blogs.

I don't.

There's discipline in a print column. It has a frequency to follow. It must be the right length. It must make deadline. It must be edited. Most significantly, the column is part of a greater whole – the newspaper – that's built on accuracy and fair play, not wind-blown conclusions.

Blogs will give you more than you want to know about blue states and red states and liberals and conservatives and whose campaign slush fund is tainted with ill-gotten greenbacks.

But will the posters go to Burna, Ky., as I did, and bring back a story on perhaps the world's premier backwards-speller?

Will they find their way to Mill Shoals, Ill., as I did, to meet the kindly 81-year-old janitor who had the elementary school gymnasium named for him?

Nope and nope.

End of rant.

So what's in the book?

Chasing after celebrities has never been a high priority, but I had interesting chats with Sam Snead, Tiny Tim and Eli Wallach. Their stories are sprinkled in the pages.

I volunteered at an elementary school in a poor part of Evansville. I organized a juggling club and took some of the children to places like the mall, the pet store, the playground and the museum. Few lived with both biological parents. Some of their caregivers had problems with drugs and alcohol. A few were in jail. I often wrote about the time I spent with these youngsters and include three such columns in this collection. A few days after I took one little girl out, her father was arrested for making meth and she was taken out of the home.

The time I spent with these boys and girls was unforgettable. I'm in the final stages of a book that takes a closer look at one child's day-to-day dealing with grinding poverty.

There are columns about a homeless man, a crying prostitute, laughing tornado survivors and the death of my 1994 Mercury Sable.

And columns about a veteran of three wars who almost got his nose blown off, a woman whose triplets died at birth, a man who showed up sloshed for his drunk-driving trial and the total mortification that was failing to climb the rope when I was in high school gym class.

And columns about a Freedom Rider from the early 1960s who recalls the firebombing of his bus outside Anniston, Ala., a stroke that stole the laughter from a clown, a minister who witnessed the execution of a member of his congregation, and how when you're selecting boys for your 9-year-old baseball team, it's important to consider the GLM factor (good-looking moms) because it can be a long season.

I'd like to thank the newspaper and the folks who let me tell their stories.

I hope you enjoy the book.

— Garret Mathews
— Sept. 15, 2009

BEDFORD, Va. – The National D-Day Memorial here honors the approximately 4,500 American and Allied soldiers who perished in the June 6, 1944, invasion of Nazi-occupied France.

There are plaques that list the names of the dead and explain the heroics of individual soldiers, units and ships.

A 19-foot wall of statuary shows rifle-wielding troops hanging onto each other as they scale a cliff. Beneath it, a mock-up of a beach depicts a landing craft and bronze sculptures of soldiers both fighting and dying.

A high granite arch at the entrance is named "Overlord," the code name for the invasion.

A large crowd has come to the 88-acre site this Memorial Day weekend.

A few are survivors of the Normandy onslaught.

They talk about being seasick from the six-foot waves, and how tracer rounds lit up the beach like a small city.

They talk about the twisted pieces of metal pipe the Germans put in the water to try to impede the landing that looked like upside-down jacks, and how the bodies of many of their buddies washed up on the surf.

The elderly man stares at the 12 flags of the Allied nations. He bows his head at that portion of the memorial devoted to Omaha Beach where the most GIs lost their lives.

He wasn't a part of the war in Europe. His duty station was in the Far East where he drove a truck loaded with steel girders over the Burma Road to China.

"This was our war," he says to his son. "It doesn't matter where it was fought. We were all a part."

The elderly man can only walk a few steps without losing his breath. The son is along in case he overdoes it.

They stand next to the sculpture of the clutch of soldiers climbing the faux cliff. The elderly man points out the ammo pouches and bayonets on their pistol belts.

"That's exactly how it looked down to the last detail," he says excitedly. "I was outfitted the same way except I had a carbine instead of an M1 rifle."

The elderly man focuses on the jets of air going off intermittently in the water near the sculpture of the landing craft and the accompanying sound effects.

"Machine gun fire. They got the noise just right. I heard it over my head on the Burma Road. After a while, you don't worry about it. You're either going to live or you're going to die."

The elderly man talks about how many Allied troops drowned under the weight of their 60-pound packs, and how the Germans leveled heavy fire from behind concrete fortifications they thought would never be breached.

The son knows this and other details about the assault, but says nothing. This is his father's day.

Ken Mathews is in a hurry to get to the next display.

It's a statue of a helmet hanging on the butt end of a rifle.

"This is a memorial to the dead," my father says, wheezing. "A lot of them didn't make it."

He wipes his eyes.

"Too many."

There's nothing for me, or anyone else to say.

It was his day.

BURNA, Ky. – First of all, know this: Norris McElmurry is only a high school graduate. He doesn't own a telephone, much less a computer. He's not a member of any brain-based organization. His hobby is pitching washers.

The retired house painter's only income is a Social Security check. That means no stacks of encyclopedias in the living room. No piles of dictionaries.

The 65-year-old man has never been married. He doesn't own a car and rarely strays from Burna (population about 130). The church van picks him up three times a week for services. For fun, he walks the mile to the convenience store to joke around with old friends.

McElmurry has a "gift," as he calls it. Backwards spelling. Give him any word he knows how to spell – he estimates having more than 10,000 in cold storage – and he'll send it back to you in reverse faster than an exchange of forehands in professional tennis.

The Livingston County man can do sentences and even short paragraphs.

"I can't explain it other than to say the letters just line up in my head, and I can spit 'em out rattlesnake-fast," he says, drawling. "I sure ain't got no big IQ. I'm just an old country boy."

Indeed, there's nothing fancy about this guy.

He lives in the place his parents moved into when they got married. He likes to hunt and fish. To save money in the winter, he heats only one room of the old house.

"I got into the backwards spelling when I was about 12. Never seen anybody else who could do it."

McElmurry greets visitors on the ancient porch where it's best to keep an eye out for dive-bombing wasps.

He talks about loving the Lord, and says the best advice he's ever received was "the higher up you climb in life, the more people can see your hind end. It just proves that money don't buy happiness."

Formalities over, McElmurry is ready to play the game in which he may be the world's only contestant. He leans forward in antici-pation.

"Give me a word. No, give me a bunch of words."

He has no problem with "rhinoceros." Or "procrastination." Or "psychological."

It gets better. The Preamble to the Constitution comes out in less than a minute.

The man wants to make sure his ability is taken the right way.

"I don't do this to put on airs, OK? I mean, it's not that I'm brag-ging or anything. I just do what I say I can do."

He says he never backwards-spells as fast as he can "because somebody might accuse me of leaving out a letter. That would be lying. I could never do that."

Years ago, McElmurry would read a dictionary in between house-painting jobs and visits to the convenience store.

"I don't do so much of that any more. But if I hear somebody say a word I don't know, I'll get it straight in my head. You never know. That might be the word some guy on the street tries to test me with."

He's done his thing a few times in front of civic groups, "but not all that often. Mostly all I do is stay home and watch 'The Andy Griffith Show' on TV. I like that program. It's simple, just like me."

McElmurry also is able to alphabetize words. Throw out "bron-chitis" and he goes from the "b" to the "t" in seconds.

"But the backwards spelling is what I do best. I'll probably just stick with that."

Sad End For Special Woman Who Loved Hugs

Jan Griepenstroh had a learning disability caused by the combination of chickenpox and high fever when she was a toddler.

She sometimes stuttered and had to repeat sentences. She had to study much harder than her classmates to earn passing grades.

After graduating from Heritage Hills High School, Jan enrolled at Southern Indiana Rehabilitation Services to learn employment skills.

Jan once held three jobs at one time, sometimes putting in as many as 70 hours a week at the pallet factory and the two restaurants where she was a dishwasher.

Some family members thought Jan should cut back, but were reluctant to bring up the subject. They knew about her stubborn streak, and how desperately she wanted to prove she could live on her own.

Jan enjoyed competing in the Special Olympics. Her favorite events were aquatics, track and field, and, later, bowling.

She won many medals. When she wasn't proudly wearing them, they were on display in her rental apartment in Jasper, Ind.

Jan learned to drive, but didn't trust herself in cities or unfamiliar roads. Most of her miles were logged around Jasper and to visit family members around Tell City, Ind.

The woman became interested in coaching young Special Olympics athletes. She gave talks throughout Indiana on how to be a volunteer. A favorite topic was how Special Olympics made her brave, and how you can accomplish almost anything if you try hard enough.

She was a librarian at her church and devoted parts of two days each week to help prepare material for classes.

Jan enjoyed writing poems about the hundreds of people she knew. The verses touched on their unique personalities and reflected the author's upbeat approach to life. Sometimes the poems closed with references to heaven.

Jan loved giving out hugs. It was her way of saying everything from, "Nice to meet you," to "Where have you been for so long?"

She was en route to a funeral when her car ran off Indiana 245 near Lamar.

The vehicle sank to the bottom of a 12-foot pond. When rescue personnel brought the car to the surface, Jan was dead. She was 40 years old.

At the wake, one of Jan's poems about Special Olympics was read to the packed audience. The preacher wondered aloud if there was anyone in the congregation whom the deceased hadn't hugged at least once. Almost everyone was crying.

"Jan knew she was different, but she didn't consider herself handicapped," says Litha Snyder, her sister.

Snyder recalls Jan's strong sense of family, that she telephoned almost every day to keep track of everyone's activities.

"But probably her greatest trait was how she learned to be independent. I'd like to be able to instill that in my own children."

MILL SHOALS, Ill. – Usually a gymnasium is named for a school superintendent, or a member of the board of education, or the basketball coach who put the team on the map.

Not this stretch of wooden floor.

The Mill Shoals Grade School basketball court honors an 81-year-old janitor who's been pushing brooms since 1955 and likes to wear caps that come from the tobacco warehouse.

Orin Lambert suffered a stroke 10 years ago. It's hard for him to get up from a chair. He forgets things. He walks with a limp.

But the White County man still puts in a four-hour shift most days, beginning at 6 a.m. If his battered 1976 Buick is feeling poorly, he gets up that much earlier to make sure he's not late.

The man fires the furnace, arranges the chairs in the classrooms and does everything else necessary to get ready for another school day. He has no plans to retire.

"He's such a wonderful old gentleman that the local school board and the PTO thought naming the gym for him would be a good idea," said Roger Heckler, principal of the school that has 74 students and five teachers in eight grades. "He's been here so long it wouldn't seem right to name the gym after anybody else."

The wooden sign honoring Lambert that will be mounted in the gym is still under construction. The custodian was given a plaque at a Christmas program at the school.

"There must've been 500 people present that night," the janitor recalled. "I told myself no way I was gonna make a speech and I didn't. I just sorta stood there."

Lambert grew up in Cisne, Ill., the son of a farmer. He drove his first team of horses at 13. His wife, Audrey, died when their only child was seven days old. He never remarried.

"She passed away in the night – real sudden. It hit me hard. I thought I wasn't gonna be able to keep living."

The stroke also hit at night. Orin Lambert woke up in the hospital.

"I couldn't walk and I wasn't able to say but a few words. I was off work for six months. I'm better, but I still have to go to the doctor four times a year."

He made a break from the farm and operated a poolroom in Mill Shoals. Business wasn't good and Lambert was receptive to a $35-a-week job offer to come to the grade school.

Before the stroke, his day at the school was sometimes 12 hours long. There was always something to do. If it wasn't paper on the floor, it was a mess in the cafeteria. Lambert always smiled through it.

"Being around kids all the time would make some people my age a little nervous," said the man whose school days ended in the eighth grade. "Me, it doesn't bother."

We walk to the gymnasium that Heckler says is at least 50 years old. The plaque honoring Orin Lambert will go on the stage beside the sign ballyhooing the Mill Shoals Cardinals.

"Sometimes I'll sweep in here two, three times a day. Just me, nobody else. I've had a lot of time to think over the years."

He looks at the wall that still bears the names of basketball players who played here when there was such a thing as Mill Shoals High School.

"I had no idea they were gonna call the gym after me until a few days before the Christmas program. It made me proud, but I was awful nervous. I had never heard of a building named for a custodian. I mean, how are you supposed to act?"

The boys were home for the weekend. The one who recently graduated from college and the one who just started.

Made a complete mess of things.

Clothes all over the place. Breakfast items spilled. Dirt tracked on the carpet. Computer cords all over the place. Doberman leavings on the sofa. Lunch items spilled.

Colin and Evan were particularly wanton in the bathroom.

Towels thrown in every direction. Shampoo bottles laid to waste. Doberman leavings in the bathtub. Enough water on the floor for a small craft warning.

It was great.

For too long our household has been orderly. Respectable. Quiet. What fun is that?

We needed an infusion of youngsters and their laundry and their ability to keep the bathroom mirror fogged up for hours.

I'll take your questions or comments.

Geez, your sons not only have you wrapped around their fingers, they've attached puppet strings.

And a happy marionette I am, my friend. Fatherhood has been the joy of my life. If you hear of a good deal on a time machine so I can do it all over again, send the salesman my way.

But what about the floored food and the high tide in the bathroom?

Mere details. The boys could be anywhere else, but they chose to be with us.

So you don't impose a ton of rules?

Oh, there are plenty. No ripping out the ceiling. No forcible removal of plumbing fixtures. And no explosives of any kind unless they're specifically earmarked for moles.

Towel-picker-upper sounds like a lowly profession, even for you.

Not at all. I'm doing a position paper on how post-shower males ages 18-24 require a minimum of one absorbent cloth for each appendage.

What else do you do other than squeegee excess water?

Say "Not in the least" when they ask if they're being too much of a bother.

Sounds like they're reaping all the benefits. What's in it for you?

The glow at day's end when the boys are in their beds and I'm certain – if only for this one evening – that they're safe and sound.

You sentimental old fool.

Sue me.

Is there any parenting advice you'd like to share?

Your children are only this age once. The clock from kidhood to adulthood is ticking and when it goes off it's like a bomb. You can't defuse it. You can't change the setting. Let your domicile be the center of childhood activity in the neighborhood. Sleeping bags, water pistols, baseball gloves, the works.

Stage regular romps in your living room. Remember, in the overall scheme of things, spilled macaroni and cheese isn't all that important.

When are the boys coming back for another visit?

Two weeks. The washing machine has requested steroids.

Are you planning anything special?

I'm thinking about making a giant "Welcome" sign in the front yard made out of shampoo bottles. Underline it with foam from the carpet cleaner.

You're just an old softie.

Sue me.

August 29, 1994
Stroke Steals Laughter From Billy The Clown

PRINCETON, Ind. – Billy Griffin positions the wheelchair so he can look out the window of the convalescent center. He pays particular attention to the cars speeding by.

"I miss the travel most of all," the 74-year-old man says sadly. "The hardest part of all is just sitting here."

Griffin was a professional clown for more than 40 years. The Fort Branch, Ind., native hit the big time, one doing his white-face act for shows put on by Clyde Beatty and Ringling Brothers. He bought a Ford Thunderbird and took his place in the caravan behind the elephant trucks.

There were smaller circuses, too, like Hoxie and the Adams Brothers. He rarely stayed with a show longer than two or three seasons. Sometimes he didn't care for the boss, Other times he just wanted a change of scenery. The only state he missed was Maine.

Billy the Clown, as he was known, suffered a stroke six years ago in Iowa. He couldn't care for himself, so he moved back to his native Gibson County. He is no longer able to walk and has only limited use of his hands. The false teeth don't fit properly and he struggles to make himself understood.

"I don't have any complaints. All my life I wanted to be a tramp. I pretty much got my wish."

He was born with curvature of the spine. The stroke made the condition worse.

"The best job for me in the circus would have been bareback rider, but my back made that impossible. The only things left were doing contortion acts and being a clown."

He would squeeze inside a tiny car and get laughs when he popped out beside a much larger clown. The crowd also guffawed when he dressed as a woman en route to the altar and a poodle walked on the train of the long dress.

Griffin worked with Emmett Kelly, perhaps the world's best-known clown. Several times he was on the same bill as the Flying Wallendas, a famous high-wire act.

Sometimes he made extra money putting up handbills or helping with wardrobe. It came in handy. The most he earned in the ring was $300 a week.

"Growing up, people would always stare at me because of my back. It didn't bother me much after I started with the circus. There, when they got their look, it was all part of the act."

He joined the Mills Brothers Circus at Poseyville, Ind., after graduating high school. After five years of selling popcorn and doing odd jobs, he caught on with the Cole Brothers Circus in Louisville and learned the fine art of clowning.

"The job was good, but it was a grift circus and I didn't like all the gambling."

Clowns, he said, are notoriously jealous people. He remembers knock-down fights when one tried to hog the spotlight. He recalls a particularly vicious brawl over the affections of a midget woman.

"I wasn't a very tough person and didn't like the arguments so I left."

Some of the circuses he worked on had as many as 20 clowns. Some put on as many as three shows a day.

"It's a hard life, harder than most people think. They only see the time you're out in the lights."

I asked Billy the Clown if he ever tried any other line of work.

"My father took me down in his coal mine once, but I didn't think much of it. Another time I had a bad boss and I quit clowning to run a pizza stand in Arizona. That didn't work out and I ended up going back to the show."

Do you wish you were working?

"Yes, but you have to have your health for that. There's not even one part of the act I can still do. The laughs. That never gets out of your system."

My grandmother died a few days ago. She was 96.

The lady lived almost her entire life in a paper mill town deep in the mountains of Western Virginia where her husband was a welder.

There was no need for a car. Everything necessary to sustain life was right there. Factory. Presbyterian Church. The clothing store where she worked. And, if an emergency came up and travel was involved, the bus station.

Ruby and Walter had a simple, almost 19th-century existence. Spent their days earning a few bucks. Sat on the porch at night with the neighbors and talked about who was sick, who received his foreman's papers and whose sweet corn hadn't come in yet.

If you weren't feeling well, Ruby was at the your door with a pie. You probably got one if you made foreman, too.

The lady was always giving things away. If she heard you didn't have enough clothes, she'd go through her closet. Walter's, too. He never complained about looking for a pair of socks and finding his drawer only a shadow of its former self. It was all part of living with Ruby.

After she was taken to the rest home, we bought her all kinds of dolls and stuffed animals. We later learned she gave them to residents who didn't have anything pretty in their rooms.

Ruby developed dementia in the last years of her life. She confused my father with Walter who died in 1973. She switched my brother and me, and couldn't remember what I did for a living or where I did it.

I eventually accepted her loss of memory and steered the conversation toward things that happened before I was born. On good days, Granny had vivid recollections about the ration coupon booklets of the Second World War.

But I went through a time I'd like to forget. It upset me that a grandmother of mine was unable to keep track of names. I thought what she needed was repetition. Enough practice, I thought, and she could reel off the information without flubbing up.

Visits turned into memory drills.

"Hello, Granny."

"Oh, how are you, Dan?"

"I'm not Dan. I'm Garret."

"Where do you live?"

"In Evansville, Granny."

"I thought it was Abingdon."

"No, Granny. That's where my brother Dan lives. Remember: Garret is Evansville, Indiana. Dan is Abingdon, Virginia."

"Is Dan the one who works at the newspaper?"

"No, Granny. That's Garret. It's easy to keep us apart. Dan is insurance. Garret is newspaper."

"And where does Garret live?"

"In Indiana, Granny, Evansville."

"Well, I think that's so nice. Walter came to see me today."

"No, he didn't, Granny. Walter is dead. Your son came to visit."

"What's his name?"

"Kenneth."

"Where are his boys? I never see them any more."

"His boys are Garret and Dan. They're right here."

"I thought Dan was dead."

"No, Granny. Walter is dead. Your husband is dead. Your two grandchildren are fine."

"Well, I think that's so nice."

On and on the drill went until some family member tapped me on the shoulder and told me to give it a rest.

I finally was able to. I wish it hadn't taken so long.

Maybe you have an elderly relative with a failing memory.

Don't do what I did.

Have them remember the pies.

Not names.

Drills are for the armed services.

Not loved ones.

Once upon a time in this football fairy tale, there was a senior in high school named Golden Boy who could run like the very wind with a pigskin tucked against his numeral.

He could sidestep five tacklers with a single swivel of his hips. Likewise, he could carry five books under his arm without losing his balance. He exceeded his goal of making an "A" for every touchdown scored.

Golden Boy dated Janie May, the president of the Chemistry Club. Her father, a fat-cat corporate lawyer, told his daughter she could have a Corvette, but she said she'd rather walk to class.

Golden Boy kept a scrapbook of clippings, but none about his gridiron exploits. Instead, it was full of articles about Marco Polo and William the Conqueror that he thought he might need in college.

Golden Boy never sat at the back of the classroom with his feet propped up on the desk. He kept his book turned to the right page and asked probing questions. He tutored students who fell behind.

Head Football Coach of Major University made a recruiting trip to Golden Boy's house. They talked a few minutes about the spread offense, but spent most of their time discussing the nation's trade deficit. Bowl games weren't mentioned. Neither was Golden Boy's future in the National Football League.

We're first and foremost about academics, Head Football Coach said. The game is secondary to our players getting their degrees.

For real? Golden Boy asked.

You bet, said Head Football Coach, who taught four classes and begged the academic dean to give him more work.

Golden Boy asked Head Football Coach if he could visit the campus, that he was looking forward to continuing their discussion about Iran's place in the nuclear weapons scheme of things. Coach said, by all means, and be sure to bring your stack of Time magazines so we can swap out with my stack of Newsweeks.

When Golden Boy arrived at Major University, he was impressed by the many computer work stations in the athletic dorm, and the extensive collections of Kierkegaard and Nietzsche that Head Football Coach kept on his bookshelf.

He said, OK, I'll sign. You'll never regret it, Head Football Coach said.

Golden Boy never missed a class while at Major University. Never appeared on the police blotter. Never asked the booster club for a penthouse suite.

Golden Boy never wore jewelry or bandannas or headbands or anything else that would call attention to him at the expense of the team.

When Golden Boy scored a touchdown, he simply handed the football to the referee. He believed it was his job to score touchdowns, and that he shouldn't stage wild celebrations in the end zone for doing what he was supposed to do.

Some of Golden Boy's teammates enjoyed wearing commando-style clothing with camouflage paint and pistol belts. They believed such outfits made them big shots at the nightclubs downtown.

Golden Boy chastised his teammates. Good football players don't make a spectacle of themselves, he told them. Good football players dress for success, not basic training.

Ashamed, his teammates took the military gear back to the Army surplus store. They agreed they wanted to be big shots in world cultures class, not at the nightclubs downtown.

When Golden Boy graduated, the president of Major University referred to him as a student-athlete.

Nobody laughed.

Golden Boy married Janie May. Her father said he could get them high-paying, mindless jobs with a huge corporation, but they turned him down to teach at an inner-city elementary school.

Golden Boy and Janie got 11 hugs the first day and twice that many the next.

And they lived happily ever after.

OWENSBORO, Ky. – The Rev. J. David Wells watched from the front row as the man who became his friend died.

Larry Joe Johnson was led into the death chamber at the Starke, Fla., prison. Two guards strapped him into the electric chair. A metal cap was placed on top of his head. The condemned man made eye contact with the minister, and seemed to smile as the black hood was draped over his shoulders.

The executioner pulled a lever that gave life to 2,000 volts of electricity. Larry Joe Johnson stiffened in the three-legged chair, and then slumped as smoke seeped from the bottom of his pants. Wells and the other 19 witnesses were led from the room. At the gate, they saw a white hearse and two funeral home attendants.

"I was wiped out physically," Wells said. "It was very painful for him. That's a terrible, cruel way to die."

Johnson, a native of McLean County, Ky., was found guilty of shooting a 67-year-old gasoline station clerk during a 1979 robbery that netted $150. The execution ended more than 13 years of legal wrangling during which time he received four death warrants and an equal number of reprieves.

Wells, 51, pastors the 1,000-member Good Shepherd Church in Owensboro. Johnson attended the church from 1976 until 1979 when he and a 17-year-old female acquaintance suddenly left for Florida.

"He was adopted at a very young age by an aunt and uncle who went to our church. We socialized several times and I found Larry a very likable person. He was always on the move, a big talker. We had a big fund-raising drive and he bought a pew. We hit it off well. I considered us friends."

Johnson served two tours of duty in Vietnam. After his discharge, he joined the Kentucky National Guard where he suffered a head injury from a smoke grenade explosion. He was granted a psychiatric disability.

"I can't speak for his life before he started coming to our church and I can't explain what happened in Florida," the minister went on. "All I can say is that while he attended our church, he was the kind of man who never met a stranger."

Johnson went to prison in Kentucky for shooting his wife during an argument. He was seeing a parole officer when he started going to Good Shepherd.

"The man struck me as someone who had been shell-shocked by what happened in Vietnam. While he was frequently amusing, he was also nervous and uptight about a lot of things. He didn't have a job and, in my opinion, there was no way he could have held one."

At trial, Johnson said he fired at the elderly clerk in a reflex reaction after he saw the man's hand move suddenly. Three psychological trauma experts testified that he suffered from post-traumatic stress disorder.

Wells made numerous trips to Florida to be with his former parishioner.

"I wanted to be there in the good times and the bad times. I wasn't going to allow the distance to be a limitation."

He saw Johnson every day during the last week of his life. Until the night of the execution, all the visits were behind a glass partition.

"At the end, he was peaceful and serene. He didn't want to die, but he accepted the fact that it was going to happen. I read Scripture while he took four or five bites of barbecue beef and slaw. The last thing we did before they came to prep him was drink a can of Mountain Dew together."

I asked the minister if he received any fallout over his decision to spend so much time with a convicted murderer.

"Nobody said a word about me being gone. They understand that Christianity is a story of grace."

The father of the groom sits in the hot sun, bedecked in brown suit and brown shoes that make him look like an elongated Fudgsicle.

Groom's orders. No running shoes at the nuptials. No clothing items that aren't of the three-piece variety and of matching color.

So polyester it is.

The mother of the groom dabs her eyes with a Kleenex.

A few feet away, their firstborn shares center stage with a wonderful young lady whose cheerfulness should be put in the water supply.

The rings are presented. Husband-and-wife-to-be lock hands. The minister finds her place in the text.

Won't be long now.

The father of the groom is determined to get through this without crying.

Hey, it's just a simple exchange of vows in front of 200 people, too many camerapersons to count and a videographer who acts like he's making Ben-Hur.

Nothing to get waterlogged about.

And the announcement of the wedding certainly wasn't a surprise. They've been together since early high school.

But the odds are against the sentimental father of the groom holding it together.

He's too much "Remember when?" and, "Gee, it seems like only yesterday."

He looks at the Super 8 film of the groom asleep in his stroller outside the Chicago zoo.

He looks at scorebooks he saved back when the groom played kids' baseball.

He treasures the pictures taken when the groom beat on his drums in the basement.

The father couldn't be prouder of his first-born.

The young man is responsible, sure of himself, and good at the computer-laying-on-of-hands that he does for a living.

"You're too quiet," the mother of the groom asks. "Sure you're OK?"

The father of the groom nods.

It's the heat, he explains. The brown suit feels like a truck motor that's been running hot since the Reagan administration. A few more degrees and the brown shoes can achieve liftoff.

The bride and groom go off to one side.

Probably to stick their heads into an icebox.

But no. They get out a dozen red roses and walk toward their parents.

The father of the groom feels his lips tremble.

Colin gives six roses to his mother.

"Thanks for everything," he says.

No Kleenex, no matter how reinforced, can hold up under these circumstances.

She cries.

Colin gives six roses to his father.

"Thanks for being there for me."

Several sentences form in his mind, but none come out.

The father quits fighting it.

And cries.

Warning: This column contains biting commentary.

Feb. 13. 3 a.m.

Lt. David Turpen and patrolman Scott Steward of the Henderson, Ky., Police Department respond to a domestic violence call.

I'll let the 40-year-old Turpen, a 15-year veteran of the force, take it from here.

"You could tell something had been going on. The woman had a scratch under her eye. We did our interviews and the man who was with her (Lavon Cabell) admitted there had been a scuffle. There was some drinking.

"Under Kentucky's domestic violence law, we're required to make an arrest if there are physical signs of injury. We informed Mr. Cabell that he was going to jail.

"At first, he didn't have a problem with that. He took out his billfold and said he wanted to count his money before we took him away. We were patient and watched him count the bills three times. Each time it came to $190.

"Finally, Scott reached over to put the handcuffs on, and that's when the punching started. They were rolling around on the living room bed for a few seconds and then Mr. Cabell got on top. I jumped in to break it up, and in the process my hand went across Mr. Cabell's face.

"That's when he bit me on the ring finger of my right hand. He clamped down as hard as he could for at least a minute. I've never experienced such intense pain in my life. Shock had to be coming on. All I could think of was to holler at Scott over and over that I was sorry I couldn't be more help, but this guy had hold of my finger and there wasn't anything I could do. And this was all happening with me wearing Kevlar gloves that are supposed to be knife-proof.

"Finally, I was able to break his grip and we got some more officers to the scene. There was still a little bit of struggle, but they were able to subdue him. One of the policemen noticed the glove I had been wearing. As he lifted it, a three-quarter-of-an-inch section of finger fell out."

The emergency room doctor trimmed the bone that was sticking out and sewed the wound. Re-attachment of the fingertip wasn't considered because of the risk of infection.

"I dislocated my shoulder once, and I've had a few scrapes trying to arrest people, but nothing like this," Turpen said.

And then there was the guff he had to take at the station house.

"I'm one of the more morbid ones, so I knew I was gonna hear about it. There was the joke about me getting a 10 percent discount for a manicure. One guy said if I'd go out to his truck with him, he had a tip for me. And there have been a lot of references to finger food."

He apologized for not showing me the ill-fated digit, saying he had just put on a fresh sterile gauze.

"But I've got pictures," he offered.

I begged off, glad to be in a profession that affords incredibly good odds that I'll finish a shift with the same number of fingers as when I started.

BURNT PRAIRIE, Ill. – James Ralph Cash sits alone in the house he's lived in since 1937, alternately doing crossword puzzles and adjusting the oxygen tubes he needs to survive.

"I have so many spells where I just can't breathe. Sometimes I wonder how many more minutes I have left."

He has emphysema from four decades of smoking cigarettes.

"When I'm pushing my oxygen tank around in public, I'm not shy about coming to people who are lighting up. I ask if they want to end up like me."

James Ralph was a school bus driver and janitor for many years in this corner of White County. He's known as a mostly self-taught piano player, rarely missing a service at the Cumberland Presbyterian Church.

The 76-year-old man never married and gets homesick when he strays too far from tiny Burnt Prairie.

His cluttered house is filled with clocks, books, manual typewriters, potted plants and puzzle magazines. There's a piano and a pump organ that are the stuff of museums.

It's the top of the hour. Dozens of wind-up clocks go off at once. The several cuckoos are a few seconds late, but make up for it in volume.

"I collect 'em. I don't how many I have, but I'd know if one was missing."

James Ralph looks at the vintage pump organ. Melancholy sets in.

"I can't play it anymore," he says, tapping the oxygen tubes. "Too much exertion. I just give out. Nobody knows how awful this is."

He plays some hymns on the piano. His fingers fly over the keys.

"During the WPA days years ago, they sent a woman to town to give lessons for three months. I wasn't interested at the time, but Dad made me go. That's the only real training I've ever had."

James Ralph drives to Fairfield, Ill., for groceries and to play dominos at the gun club. Sundays are for church. Saturday nights are for practicing for the next day's music.

Other than that, he's a homebody.

"If I don't pick up my mail, the lady at the post office comes by to see if I'm dead."

He plays a lot of solitaire in addition to doing the puzzles, some of which he can finish in less than 20 minutes. It makes him mad when he can't figure out a clue.

"I've about read myself crazy with books, so I should know."

James Ralph Cash leads the way to the player piano.

"When I got it, the thing wouldn't work at all. I tuned it and was in seventh pig heaven. Now it's back to where it was before, and I'm too bad off to do anything about it."

He winces. His chest hurts.

"It's tragic when you can't breathe. Tragic."

Thirty years ago today, I packed my worldly possessions into a Ford Pinto and took off down the road for my first newspaper job at the Bluefield Daily Telegraph. Because I wasn't very worldly, I only needed half the trunk.

I arranged to live in a boarding house. The eightysomething owner said we would get along just fine.

There were just a few rules.

I would pay the week's $10 rent on Saturday no earlier than 9 a.m. before she was properly dressed. And no later than 11 a.m. when she left for the bank.

I could not do anything that could even remotely be construed as noise.

I could not use the hall telephone longer than 60 seconds. An egg timer was beside the receiver as a reminder.

I could only use one towel a day.

"This is a place of residence, not a laundry," she liked to say.

And I couldn't bring women up to my room.

"Morals of this country are going to the devil," she said, fanning herself with a church bulletin. "If I can help just one boy from going bad..."

I wanted to go bad in the worst way, but living on the newspaper's $90 a week was as much as giving me a Good Conduct Medal.

I looked around my room. Bed, desk, mirror, cabinet, Book of Psalms, closet, decorative urn of Noah leading the animals into the ark and two washcloths carefully folded to look like praying hands.

The Vienna Sausages I had for lunch were working on me. I went in the bathroom, sat on the commode and contemplated my future.

Suddenly, the woman burst in.

I tried to cover up, but my shirt was too short.

"Where are you from anyway?"

Stammering and embarrassed, I told her.

"Do you know the Pullams? Bob and Jane. They're from down that way."

Desperately, I began making grunting and straining noises, hoping to get her to leave.

"Real nice people. Never miss a worship service."

She looked at her watch.

"Got to make supper. Don't forget to wash your hands."

I had just enough time to take a bath before going to the newspaper office. The knobs looked like they had been installed during the Roaring Twenties, so I didn't expect much. But to my surprise, hot and cold surged out of the respective taps.

I lathered up and hoped I hadn't forgotten to pack my Gregg Typing Manual. If I couldn't impress my co-workers with my brains, I could at least get them to appreciate my keystrokes.

I looked down at my feet. They were bright red.

There was no pain, so it couldn't be blood. I leaned over and saw Ragu Sauce coming up the drain. Lots of it.

I quickly used up my towel allotment. The rest of the dry-off was with an undershirt.

"You've got to do something about the bathtub," I said, storming into the kitchen. "My legs look like dinner."

"Oh, it's those darn pipes again."

She explained that the plumbing in the sink is connected to the plumbing in the bathtub. When stuff goes down the one, the stuff sometimes comes up the other.

"I'll pray on it, and if that doesn't work, I'll call the man next door."

That night, I wrote headlines on briefs about the Old Guard and the Bluewell Public Service District.

Occasionally my pants legs rode up. My co-workers laughed and called me "Red Man."

I was on my way.

You're taking a bunch of fifth-graders home from the pet store and the mall. They live on the poor side of town and don't have many opportunities to go places.

You get a good feeling from providing an experience the children would otherwise not have. At one time or another, you've taken out most of the kids in the class.

You hope that a few will break the cycle of poverty. You constantly push the importance of reading and working hard in school.

The odds are against them. Many of these youngsters live in inadequate, overcrowded public housing units. Many family members abuse drugs and alcohol. Some are in jail.

Only a few reside with both biological parents. More than a few are shuffled back and forth among relatives best able to come up with the month's rent money.

You ask the bright-faced little girl in the front seat what she wants to be when she grows up.

The words come out with no hesitation.

Heart surgeon.

And not because she happened to see a doctor show on TV the night before. The child says she's been interested in medicine for a long time because that's the best way to help people.

You explain that she'll have to go to college for many years to be a physician.

She nods.

You tell her the school will be hard and she'll have to study long hours.

She knows that, too.

You tell her she'll make a fine doctor. The world can always use people who want to help others.

The little girl says no one in her family has had a job even close to a doctor. She says it will be really neat to be the first.

This is wonderful. The first step in making a dream come true is having one.

You turn onto the pothole-filled street where the bright-faced little girl lives.

Music blasts from a stereo. The lyrics aren't suitable for a fifth-grader's ears.

A black car takes a couple of slow laps around the block before coming to a halt. A suspicious-looking man approaches the driver's side window. The window is rolled down. The man sticks his head in. It looks like a drug deal.

An older man staggers out from behind a Dumpster carrying a bottle in a brown paper bag. A woman standing outside one of the battered apartment units cusses another woman who responds in kind.

It's a snapshot in the lives of people mired in both poverty and hopelessness.

The bright-faced little girl says she can't wait for tomorrow.

You try to guess what she's looking forward to.

Something at school?

She shakes her head.

Something at church.

She shakes her head.

You give up.

Tomorrow, she explains, is the day her family gets their food stamps.

You wave a weak goodbye as the bright-faced little girl opens the dirty door of one of the apartments.

A dream has met reality.

The telephone rings. It's Dick Peterson, drummer for the Kingsmen.

"Heard you've been trying to get hold of me," he says.

I have more than 300 records and tapes, mostly from the '60s and '70s. The Kingsmen are in the mix.

But there's something else, I tell the guy. A bus could run over me tomorrow, severing every organ. I absolutely cannot be placed on that cold slab without interviewing a member of the group that gave the world, "Louie, Louie."

The old and the new, I tell him. Fill me in.

"We finally had our day in front of the judge," Peterson says. "It went all the way to the Supreme Court, but they upheld the ruling governing ownership of the old master tapes. It took nine years, but we finally own all our recordings."

How did you get in the group?

"The Kingsmen got started in the late 1950s with bongo drums and folk music. I came around in 1963 when they had more of a Ventures sound. I was in the high school library with Norm's (Sundholm, the bass player) girlfriend. She told me the band was being rearranged because some guys were going into the military, and that I should try out for drummer.

"The group was making $20 a week playing at grocery-store openings, and that was good money so I said, sure. I later learned I got the job because I played louder than anybody else."

Enough small talk. Tell me about "Louie, Louie."

"(Lead singer) Lynn Eaton's dad heard about a cruise line that liked our music, so he paid $36 an hour for a recording studio. 'Louie' was one of four songs we sang and the only one we did twice. The first time, they said the vocal was too loud. The conditions were pretty primitive. The engineers couldn't change the mix, so all we could do was move the microphone around. You had less vocal and more junk, but that's the version that was put out."

You never re-mastered it?

"That's right. There were mistakes in the guitar parts, but we figured it didn't make any difference because nobody would ever hear it."

But then the FBI stepped in and said the dirty lyrics were corrupting America's youth.

"Yes, and that's when we had a hit. The song was banned in January of 1964 and two months later, it was up to No. 2. You tell people they can't buy a record and that's exactly what they're gonna do."

And were the lyrics dirty?

"Lord, no. It was just a Jamaican sailing song. Some of the words were hard to understand because of the way it was recorded. We were just a bunch of kids. No drugs. No drinking. We weren't trying to pull anything over on anybody. Besides, art doesn't lead a people. It's a reflection of the people."

How was it to have the FBI on your case?

"Hilarious. They followed us everywhere and sat in on our shows. Spot 'em a mile away. The only ones in black suits. They started a rumor that we played in Saran Wrap and jockstraps. And this from a man (J. Edgar Hoover) who went around wearing a dress."

You guys finally got unbanned, right?

"Yeah. The judge said 'Louie' was unintelligible at any speed."

What got you in trouble in the 1960s would be nothing today. There's f-this and m-f that. Do you think it's gone too far?

"I believe in freedom of speech, but not in language that insults people," Dick Peterson says. "Some of the music today creates less respect for humans. You can say a lot and make your point without going all the way off the wall."

Susan Burton opens the door of her cheap motel room.

"Look around," the 38-year-old Evansville woman says. "This is what homeless looks like."

Cans of green beans are on a table, courtesy of relief agencies. A few changes of clothes on coat hangers. A few bus tokens. A hot plate donated by the motel.

I ask about habits.

"Whiskey and cocaine. I admit it," the thin woman says as she lights a cigarette. "But not any more. I swear."

I ask about her children.

"The oldest is 15. He's autistic and he's got asthma and curvature of the spine. We've moved five times in the last year and that's made it pretty rough with him at school."

She says the youngest is 2, and has been in foster care the past year because authorities decided he was living in substandard housing.

"It liked to kill me when they took him away."

I ask about money.

Mrs. Burton laughs.

"I don't have a bank account. Let's see how much ready cash we can come up with."

She opens a change purse and dumps the contents on the bed. She sorts through the nickels and dimes.

"Maybe enough for a few Cokes."

A relative, she explains, paid for the motel through the end of the month. She hopes to go to a family shelter, but there are no guarantees.

"Financially-wise, it wasn't all that bad until two years ago. I thought the bills on my mother's house were getting paid and I found out they weren't. The debt was way up there and the only thing to do was sell the home.

"I didn't come out of it very good. I bought a 1976 Mercury, but it's not running any more. I got me a house trailer, but it started busting up when they made me move it to another lot."

She talks about trying to make ends meet on food stamps and a monthly AFDC (Aid to Families and Dependent Children) check of $229.

And how she has submitted dozens of job applications for everything from dishwasher to waitress.

And how she collected four bags of soda cans from the side of the road, "but it's a little tough on the other riders to throw all that stuff on the bus when you want to get home."

She insists the house trailer wasn't substandard housing.

"Sure, it looked a mess the day they came around, but that was because we were fumigating for roaches. I tried to tell them that, but it didn't do any good."

Many of us, I noted, only think about those homeless people who carry a bedroll and push a grocery cart from street to street. We tend to forget about those stuck in temporary or inadequate housing.

"Stuck, yeah, that's a good word for it," Mrs. Burton says.

She lights another cigarette.

"I'm not really a complainer. Never have been. But here lately has been a struggle. I'll admit that."

I ask Mrs. Burton if she ever thought she would find herself homeless.

"Never, I mean, we came from money. It's not supposed to happen to people like that, right? Ha, now I know better."

Barbara liked me. I knew. There were too many telltale signs.

Like the time in Miss Kent's arithmetic class when she walked past all the other boys to ask me for a pencil.

And the time she looked at me during reading group. It could have been the cloakroom she was sneaking a peak at, but I preferred to think she wouldn't crane her neck that much just for a bunch of winter coats.

I wasn't used to such attention. I led the sixth grade in pimples and my ears stuck out like baseball mitts.

Barbara's father owned the hardware store downtown. We 11-year-olds were just learning the ins and outs of the caste system, but knew enough to make fun of the girl whose father sold nails for a living.

She joined in the laughter and said the creaky floor reminded her of a Halloween haunted house.

My best friend Bill had already been to the movies with a girl.

Never mind that his dad drove. Never mind that he sneaked a Baby Ruth bar in his pocket because he didn't want to share it, and the thing melted before the second reel and ruined his pants.

A first date is a first date.

I was determined not to fall any further behind in this all-important matter, so I asked Barbara out.

Sorta.

My shyness quotient was even higher than my pimple count. My mother ended up telephoning her mother.

The word came down while I was watching an episode of "Dragnet." Barbara and I were on for Saturday afternoon to see "The Alamo."

I was terrified that I wouldn't know what to say, so I prepared some talking points.

The history book said Santa Anna's troops were so numerous and so brightly clad that when they attacked they looked like brigades of red ants.

I also read that one of the few survivors was Mrs. Dickenson, the wife of a young Texas officer.

Not trusting my memory, I wrote "Red Ants" and "Mrs. Dickenson" on my arm in bright red letters.

My palms dripped sweat. I worried that Barbara wouldn't enjoy the movie. I worried that the ink would run.

As it turned out, I was nervous over nothing. Talking to her was a snap. Like me, she thought Miss Kent should be put in a home. And, despite what her father did for a living, I finally encountered someone who knew less than I did about power tools.

The Mexican army was just starting its siege when I put my arm around her shoulder.

"They look just like a bunch of red ants, don't they?" I stammered.

"Yes, now that you mention it."

"See Mrs. Dickenson there. Well, don't worry about her dying with the others. I happen to know she's going to make it."

"Thanks for telling me."

The red ants were all over the place. The Alamo fell and a tearful Mrs. Dickenson was led from the mission.

"I had a good time," Barbara said as we walked to the hardware store.

Suddenly, she stopped me and kissed me on the cheek. I babbled incoherently for the rest of the day.

First dates will do that to a person.

Decades passed.

The telephone rings. It's my mother. Barbara is dead. Cancer.

I remembered the Saturday afternoon the Alamo fell, and how a cute little blonde-headed girl was in the seat next to me, and how my arm went to sleep around her shoulder, and how wonderful it felt.

And didn't have much to say to anybody for the rest of the day.

Friend Took Care of 'Tennessee' In Life And Death

Harold "Tennessee" England, 71, was buried this week. A dozen or so people came to the memorial service. The minister talked about the lonely and the need for compassion.

Tennessee drank.

A lot.

"Beer, liquor, wine – whatever he could get hold of," says Reuben Arnold. "All day and all night. He'd get in the back yard and sing those Merle Haggard songs loud as he could. Neighbors would holler."

The 78-year-old Arnold was Tennessee's friend. Prepared a place in the garage where he could sleep. Turned an old barrel into a bathtub. Bought him clothes.

"Last six months was the worst," the Evansville man says. "Drank even more and got to where he wouldn't bathe."

Arnold, a retired construction worker, needs an oxygen tube for his emphysema. He has heart trouble and it hurts to walk. He doesn't think he has long to live.

"I think Tennessee would still be around if I wasn't in the hospital the last few weeks. While I was laid up, I guess he did a lot of walking around, sleeping where he could."

When Tennessee was found dead, Arnold's dog Angel was by his side.

"That old critter loved him even more than me. Tennessee'd leave of the morning, and the dog would trail behind like that's where it was supposed to go."

Arnold met Tennessee 30 years ago when his friend was painting houses.

When the man was sober, Arnold says, he was sensible and pleasant to be around.

"But drunk, he'd give you a good cussing. Steal his quart of beer and he'd really let you have it."

Arnold points up the street.

"Many times I've seen him waving a bottle and trying to direct traffic. For a while, the police would take him to the drunk tank, but the last three or four years they'd just bring him home to me."

We walk to Arnold's garage. A makeshift bunk is in the corner.

"There it is, just as Tennessee left it. I got him a radio and a little TV that worked pretty good. I found an old refrigerator and when I got a little extra money, I'd put some beer in there for him. He was harmless. There was no real meanness to him."

Tennessee had his own key to the garage.

House rules?

"You weren't gonna tell that man nothing," Arnold says, laughing. "He did what he wanted."

His main hangout was Riverside Drive. Several people in that area routinely gave Tennessee their spare change, hoping at least some of it would go for food.

I asked Reuben Arnold about their friendship.

Why he took in a lodger who could be a pain. Why he put up with the Merle Haggard renditions at 3 a.m.

Part of the answer lies in strong drink. Arnold knows what it's like to be in jail with a buzz-on, although these days his focus is on the Lord and providing for his children.

And he had a way of soothing Tennessee with words.

"I could talk with him…get him to do things other people couldn't. He trusted me. That don't come easy."

Tennessee was buried in a suit from his closet.

"I would've gone to the funeral, but this…" Arnold looks at the breathing tube. "I just couldn't."

He wants to do one more thing for his friend while he's still got his strength.

"I'm gonna try, through the help of God, to get him a headstone. It'll say, 'Earl England, Better Known As Tennessee.' I'll talk to the business owners on Riverside and see if they can chip in. The man lived and he ought to be remembered."

February 2, 2006
Racism's Rough Edges Softened Over Time

Dear Benny.

Greetings from one Abingdon High School class of 1967 refugee to another.

How have you been, pal?

Our lives haven't exactly been on a parallel course. You chose the military for a career and I didn't.

But I can understand why you wanted to get out of Dodge.

As you know, our corner of the world didn't rush to integration.

Virginia waited until 1965 to put an end to the busing of black students as far as 40 miles so you could attend the inferior regional high school with the broken windows.

When you and other kids of color walked through the double doors of our high school that first day, it wasn't to a standing ovation.

Since the Confederate war memorial had been planted on the courthouse lawn, and even before, our hometown's school system had been all white.

Blacks represented change, Benny, and the prospect wasn't thrilling.

Many of us wanted our band's trumpet section to remain the same.

And our student government association.

And our homecoming court.

Caucasian.

We lined the halls. You and a dozen or so black enrollees walked a gauntlet of silence to the principal's office and then to your lockers.

We were told not to say anything under threat of expulsion, but there was no rule against murmuring.

Of course, it all worked out in the end.

You guys were great classmates. We decorated the homecoming court together. Dissected cats together. Made fun of the 139-year-old librarian together.

You were the only black guy on our high school's football team.
I remember how isolated you must have felt.
And lonely.
But you toughed it out. Even scored a few touchdowns.
Hey, pal, anybody who could lead a platoon of guys in Vietnam isn't going to let a little thing like skin pigment get him down.
I want to share something that happened the other night, Benny.
The flick, "Glory Road," is the story of the 1966 Texas Western basketball team that won the national title.
The championship game was the first in NCAA men's basketball history that five blacks were in the starting lineup.
The Miners were the definite underdogs against Adolph Rupp's all-white Kentucky squad. They had the bloodlines. They had the headlines.
Texas Western's rousing victory put an end to the myth that black athletes couldn't compete on the big stage.
I was in the movie theater with about 50 people. A few kids. A few young couples. A few folks my age. A few retirees.
All Caucasian.
Guess what happened at the end of the film, pal?
A loud cheer. No, check that. Almost a roar.
I thought of the morning you and the other black kids came to our school for the first time.
We murmured out of fear.
Forty years later, there's a movie about black basketball players who beat the odds.
And we hollered out of joy.
I thought about how far society has come since we were kids.
And walked out the theater feeling pretty good.

He Finds A $2,000 Way To Help Uncle Sam

EQUALITY, Ill. – Bill Baldwin is not a man who has a spare $2,000.

The Gallatin County widower lives alone in a small house that's almost as old as he is. He hand-rolls Velvet tobacco from a tin that's never far from his side. He wears hopelessly wrinkled work shirts. He drives a dented Ford. He talks about the things he liked to do back when he had his health – farming, trapping, squirrel-hunting.

So why did he give $2,000 to the Department of the Treasury to help retire the public debt?

"I love the United States of America and that's the truth of it. I've had me a big time in my 77 years. This country's been good to me and I wanted to give something back."

Two years ago, Baldwin read an article in a magazine about the national debt. The story said the amount was closing in on $3 trillion. The story said Congress keeps raising the debt limit. The story said it's a subject most Americans don't like to think about.

"I took stock of my situation. My sisters were doing OK and my stepchildren were doing OK. I've always felt that if people are doing good, you leave them alone. I had a little bit of money from where I sold a trailer and some farmland, so I figured I might as well give it to the government."

Baldwin talks about growing up on Saline Creek.

"If you got tired of swimming and fishing, you could watch the four passenger trains and two freight trains that came through every day. I never had a lot of big dreams. I was happy doing the little things."

And about a hobo trip he and a friend took in the 1930s.

"We just took off, didn't tell our parents or nothing. We rode one train after another until we got to California. We walked on the beach awhile and then we turned around and came back. It was two months of hobo jungles and bumming money. The job situation wasn't any better when we returned to Illinois, but at least we had done something."

He was hauling mine timbers for $3 a load when the Second World War broke out.

"That's when my life started going downhill. I caught TB in my right lung and they thought I was gonna die. The hospital did a pretty good job of curing me, but I've never been able to work much since. I piddled around some on the farm, but mostly I just sat around."

Baldwin shows the thank-you letter he received from the Treasury Department.

It says, "Your donation and interest in the financial affairs of our country are appreciated."

That's it. Not even a souvenir postcard of the Jefferson Memorial.

Didn't you at least expect to get some discount tourist coupons or something?

He shakes his head.

Did you tell the government how you wanted your money spent?

"They can do whatever they want. Give it to people on welfare if that's what pleases them. I'm not the kind of man who puts rules on the money he gives away."

Why put a drop in the fiscal bucket? Why not hold back until a few million other Americans agree to fork over?

"We're all different and we all see things differently. I don't tell anybody what to do and they don't tell me."

Our 7-year-old son, Colin, loves to play baseball. He rides his bicycle. He collects bugs. He already knows how to spell "forget."

An outstanding little boy. His parents are very lucky.

Sometimes when I see his happy face, I can't help but think about a baby girl who wasn't so fortunate. Her name was Donna Marie Stanley. She died the day Colin was born in the Bluefield hospital.

She was buried with a lock of hair from each parent, a baby rattle, a fuzzy lamb that was a present from her aunt and a stuffed dog named Droopy.

Donna Marie lived for 18 hours and three minutes.

I joined my wife in her hospital room a few hours after Colin was born. The nurses said she was a real tiger in the delivery room. They said the boy was a champ, too.

Mary Stanley's room was two doors down. I heard the young woman ask why the dead baby had to be hers. She said she hadn't done anything bad during her pregnancy. She cried, uncontrollably at first and then in a towel. Her quiet husband looked at his shoes. The doctor shook her head.

MaryAnne asked that the curtains be opened so she could see the sunshine. She telephoned everybody she could think of to tell about our beautiful Colin.

Mrs. Stanley turned out the only light in her room. She put the pillow partway over her head to make things even darker. The priest said a few words and left. He was staring at his shoes, too.

A nurse brought the baby to my wife. The boy tried to open his eyes, but wasn't having much luck. His red face felt like a sponge. His arms were hopelessly wrinkled. He looked wonderful.

Mrs. Stanley asked to see her child. A nurse returned with a form that was lost inside a pink blanket.

I took pictures of MaryAnne holding our boy. She gathered her strength and took pictures of me the same way. Colin posed willingly and even gestured with pink fingers for effect.

Mrs. Stanley spent the afternoon with her quiet husband. The nurses were careful not to make happy talk when walking past her door. An occasional cooing filled the hallway when the nursery door opened. That couldn't be helped.

I'll never forget that morning, and how our joy was dulled by another family's sadness. I often think how I would have reacted had the circumstances been reversed. I'm not sure I could have handled it.

In 1986 – a year before we moved to Evansville – the Stanleys went to Jacksonville, N.C., where Mary and Ray are both teachers. They have three boys, but no girls.

I telephoned Mrs. Stanley. We talked about Donna Marie.

"I think about her at least once a day, especially when I see a little girl at the school who is real petite and has long, curly hair. I miss her the most when there are mother-daughter functions at the school. Time puts a distance between you and what happened, but the pain is just as sharp."

The death certificate said Donna Marie Stanley died of acute respiratory distress. She was buried in the dress she would have been christened in. The undertaker took Polaroids of the child in the coffin. Mrs. Stanley keeps the pictures in a cardboard box along with other reminders that her child once lived – Donna Marie's hospital bracelet, the sympathy cards, the 100-page diary she kept of her pregnancy.

"You think about a lot of little things. Like, for example, I don't have anybody to give my wedding dress to. I saved it for all these years just to give it to my little girl when she grew up. It was the same way with my dolls. I wouldn't play with some of them when I was a child because I wanted to save them to give to my own little girl. It sounds silly, but that's what goes through your mind."

She wanted to know about Colin and I said he is doing great. She asked me to give him a hug for her.

I did.

December 23, 1991
What Do You Want For $2.99 A Minute, The Truth?

The classified advertisement in our newspaper said I could dial a 900 number and talk with a coed, a housewife or an older woman. My choice.

"Live, 1 on 1, adult," the ad went on. Just $2.99 per minute.

I called.

"Do you have a voice preference?" a nice-sounding woman asked.

Housewife, I said, trying to sound assertive.

"Please hold."

Thirty seconds of bad music.

Suddenly, my housewife came on the line.

"Hi," she purred.

I told her I've never done this sort of thing before and wasn't sure how to act. I assumed I was supposed to talk dirty.

"Most of the men do, but not all," my housewife said. "Yesterday, a guy was having a problem with his girlfriend and wanted my help."

I stammered, wasting expensive time. Then I asked her to help me with an opening line. I'll catch on, I promised. Just give me a little time to get rolling.

"A lot of guys like to start off by asking what I'm wearing."

Good idea. What are you wearing?

"Do you want the truth or the fantasy answer? The calls go about 50-50."

Both.

"OK, I'm really wearing a blue miniskirt with heels and black stockings. But if a guy wants to play, I'll tell him I don't have anything on but a black nightie."

She told me she goes by Mercedes on the phone, but that's not her real name. She said she has long blonde hair, a fair complexion and green eyes.

How do I know this? You could be fat and ugly.

"I could be, but I'm not. Besides, guys don't always tell the truth either. I had one say he's a professional baseball player."

Mercedes wouldn't tell me the name of her employer or how much money she makes. She said her office is in Atlantic City, N. J., but wouldn't say where. She said she works three days a week, two hours a day, fielding an average of eight calls per shift. She said there were 20 other women in the room taking calls.

I asked how she landed the job.

She said she answered a classified advertisement that called for "Fantasy Phone Actresses."

What if a guy gets carried away by your purring? What if he leaves hearth and home and takes off for Atlantic City?

"I tell them right off that I don't date people on the line. I explain that it's all a fantasy. Almost all of them understand."

I told Mercedes that I was beginning to feel a little more comfortable. I apologized for stammering in the early going.

"Hey, that's no problem. I have to talk a lot of guys through it."

That reminded me. I asked if she would talk dirty.

"Sure."

I had never heard such a wonderful rendition of nasty-nasty over the telephone and told her so.

She thanked me and asked if I wanted to try it.

"I'm all ears," she said, purring.

I did my best, but I'm sure she's heard better.

Don't you get tired of hearing the same old words and the same sordid suggestions?

"Not really. You pick up the phone and you never know what's going to happen."

I told her I'd better hang up, time being money. There's just one more thing. What do you tell the guys at the end?

"What else? Have a nice day."

The 45-year-old man lacks the balance to sit unaided. His legs don't work. He can't talk. He must be fed, shaved and diapered. He's almost blind.

"When I took him over, the doctors told me Thomas had cerebral palsy so bad he wouldn't live 30 days," said Anne Drury, who has raised her nephew since he was seven months old. "Now they say I've taken care of him so good he'll probably live to be an old man."

The 84-year-old Evansville woman has devoted her life to keeping Thomas alive. Keeping the child, as she calls him, has cost her a husband. It meant quitting her job. It meant thousands of hours of ironing other people's clothes to pay for his treatment and medicine.

She wants it no other way. The strong-willed woman says she has no regrets about how she has spent the last 45 years. She says she loves the child more than air.

But the woman is growing feebler by the day. She isn't sure she can care for Thomas more than another year. The thought of putting him in a nursing home gives her pain.

"It sounds bad to say, but I hope he dies before me. Nobody else will do for him like me. The only way I can know for sure he's in good hands is for him to be with God."

Anne Drury had a spinal fusion in 1960. Since 1973, she's had operations on her gall bladder, kidneys and knees. She had a tumor removed from her neck. She takes pills for her heart. It's a struggle to walk to the bus stop.

"What it boils down to is I don't want to let go of him. I know I should be looking for a place for the child to stay, but I keep putting it off. I tell myself I'm not really that bad off yet and keep plugging away."

Anne Drury said her brother was in jail when her sister-in-law gave birth to Thomas in 1945. She said her sister-in-law gave the baby to the welfare department that later placed him in a foster home. She said her late husband made her choose between him and the black-haired little boy who couldn't move his head away from his chest.

"I showed my old man the door and never let him back in my life," said the woman who never had youngsters of her own.

She coped with the convulsions and the non-stop vomiting that didn't ease until after Thomas' first birthday. She guarded him against pneumonia. She forced pieces of newspaper between his fingers until they finally uncurled.

Until the early 1970s, Anne Drury ironed shirts at 50 cents an hour. She apologized for not being able to deliver the finished product, but told her customers she couldn't leave the child. The lady earned $10 a week for taking in retarded youngsters from the rehabilitation center. She provided bed and board to elderly persons.

"I had to make a living and those were the only ways I knew how."

Why volunteer to raise a severely handicapped person who wasn't your own? Why assume the 24-hour responsibility?

"Because I have a feeling for humanity. He was in such pitiful shape and he was being treated like a kitten somebody was trying to get rid of. I decided that wasn't any way for anybody to live. I paid his bill at the foster home and we've been together ever since."

I walked in the bedroom to see Thomas. The 160-pound man makes gurgling noises like a baby. He plays with rattles. He can't turn over by himself. His food must be soft because his teeth have been removed.

"When he was little, I took him to every doctor I could think of. I exercised his little legs every night. It was my dream to see him sit up by himself, but it wasn't meant to be.

"I'll never forget the day I became his legal guardian. The judge took me aside and asked if I knew what I was getting into. He said no more than one in 10,000 persons would take on something like what I was taking on. I just shrugged my shoulders. I don't think there's anything remarkable about keeping the child so long. I'm just doing what anybody would do if they have feelings."

CALHOUN, Ky. – Willie Lee Johnson says he's healthy only when sitting down. The 68-year-old McLean County man wobbles when he walks, the lingering effect of the blow to the head he suffered in a 1975 accident.

The cane is a necessary companion, but it also serves to call attention to the sad fact that he's not the man he once was. It embarrasses him to rely on the thing. He doesn't want anyone to feel sorry for him.

The doctor told Willie Lee Johnson only a trickle of blood is flowing through an artery to his brain, a standing invitation for a stroke. The medical man said he could live to be 80 or die tomorrow.

So the patient sits more than he would like.

That's bad.

But the time spent on the living room couch opposite Hazel, his wife of 48 years, provides the perfect opportunity to hone his storytelling skills.

That's good. There's no rule that a raconteur has to hop around on a stage.

Willie Lee Johnson was a jockey from 1936 until 1956 with Ellis Park in Henderson, Ky., a frequent proving ground.

He says he once had 58 wins in a 25-day period, and 435 victories in a year's worth of riding that took him to tracks in Kentucky, Louisiana, California and New York.

He says he was a fierce competitor even in his apprentice days when he only weighed 85 pounds and would do anything—legal or otherwise—to win a race. He says when he rode in Chicago, he was the favorite jockey of gangster Al Capone.

Willie Lee laughs. Maybe his recollections are the straight dope and maybe they aren't. There's no rule that a storyteller has to provide chapter and verse.

"I don't worry about my health. I try to be happy every day and let it go at that. I'd like to go back to Ellis to see some old friends, but I left that track well-respected and I don't want 'em to see me walk and think I'm some kind of junkie. The Lord blessed me when I was racing so I got no cause to complain."

Enough sadness. On with the tales.

"It was 1939 and I was riding over at Churchill Downs. I was finally getting some good money -- $100 a week and 10 percent of what the horses earned. I was saving up to trade in my bicycle and buy a fancy new LaSalle automobile. I was feeling good 'cause I had this good horse that was going off at 27-1.

"I was heading around the turn and this other jock pulled in front of me. Whenever that happened I got so mad I couldn't stand it. I grabbed anything I could get hold of until I was able to get by. I won the race and I could just see all that big money coming, but that jock was real mad and said he was gonna claim a foul. I begged him not to 'cause I had my sights on that big car. Things got desperate and I offered him $2,500 to keep his mouth shut. That was a bad move. He not only told 'em I grabbed him, he told 'em about the $2,500. The track ended up knocking me out of action for nine months."

What about injuries? Willie Lee. Were you ever banged up?

"Sure, I was. One time I got a bad concussion, but came back to the track as soon as I could stand. I remember asking this trainer when he was gonna put me on a horse. He looked at me like I was crazy. He said, 'What's the matter with you, man? You've been riding for five days and you've had 20 winners.' I told him I couldn't remember doing it and that was the truth.

"And then there was the time this horse fell on me and I broke seven ribs, got my face torn up and ended up unconscious. They announced on the radio that I was dead and lowered the flag on the track to half-staff. Next day, the jocks came to pay their respects and you should have seen their faces when they saw me alive. They slipped me some beer in the hospital and we all had a great time."

"Little Willie," as he was called, sold Fuller brushes, worked in the oilfields and did electrical work after leaving the track. He was wiring a house in 1975 when he fell and hit his head.

Any regrets?

"Some things, but not the suspensions I got on the track. A man has to do what he thinks is right."

The morning ice on your windshield.

Scrape it off before you start to drive.

Richard was the sports editor at the West Virginia newspaper where I worked.

Never mind that he was the king of the comma splice.

Never mind that he would lose a spelling bee to a fourth-grader.

Richard was the nicest person in the world.

Nothing fancy for this guy.

Loved his two little girls. Loved listening to Dave Dudley records. Loved talking with coaches, even the ones who whined.

We only had a three-man sports staff, but Richard tried to make up for it by working 60 hours a week.

The joke was that if Richard wasn't at his desk, the managing editor should put out an APB.

The rest of us complained about the lack of the news space in the paper, and the piddling six-cents-a-mile expense policy that had to be filled out on letterhead stationery that didn't exist, and the multimillionaire publisher who drove a Bentley while we tooled around in vehicles more suited for the demolition derby.

Not Richard.

He just typed away on his 15th game story of the night, doing what he loved.

Mercer County's smaller high schools often played doubleheader basketball games at the Brushfork Armory. Sometimes I volunteered to help Richard cover them.

I enjoyed basketball and was glad to take some of the load off our hard-working sports man. But there was another reason why I was willing to donate my Saturday nights.

Something always happened.

And it usually involved Richard's car.

One night his ancient Rambler wouldn't start unless we rolled it off a hill.

Another time it wouldn't stop until he pulled the emergency

brake almost out of its socket.

Another time, this guy backed into us in the parking lot. True to his nature, instead of getting mad, Richard talked sports with him.

On this Saturday night, an ice storm hit during the games. Never one to dilly-dally getting back to the office, Richard took out his credit card and cleared off a baseball-sized opening on the windshield. Got a deadline to meet. Got to get to where I've got to be, he said.

Richard joked that he could put the car on automatic pilot and it would know how to get from the armory to the newspaper office.

Two days later, the call came to my apartment.

There had been a horrible accident on the highway the other side of Lerona. It happened around 8 a.m. A man was taking his wife to work. Their two daughters were in the back seat. It had snowed the night before. The man didn't take the time to clear his windshield. There was only a baseball-sized opening to see through. The man pulled in front of a truck that he apparently didn't see.

The children weren't badly injured. The woman suffered cuts and bruises.

The impact caved in the driver's side of the old Rambler. Richard Myers died instantly of a broken neck.

Our photographer took a picture of the debris from the mangled car that extended for more than 100 yards.

That night, I dummied in the photo on the front page and wrote the headline about my friend's death.

The ice on your windshield.

Scrape it off before you drive.

Bookmobile Lady Goes In Search Of Readers

LuAnne Riggs drives the Webster County, Ky., bookmobile truck. It contains about 2,000 copies – mostly paperbacks -- that are shelved on a slant so they won't fall on the floor in case she has to brake for a coal truck.

It's late afternoon. The schedule this day calls for her to park in Diamond. She chooses a wide spot in the road beside a vacant house.

There aren't many customers so she spends her time cataloging books.

"Some towns read more than others," Mrs. Riggs says.

The 1977 model truck has 68,000 miles. She drives it to elementary schools, day-care centers and Head Start classrooms. She also visits homebound persons who request books.

"I'll go anywhere if someone wants to read. I'm pretty determined."

The truck has spent its required hour in Diamond. Now she prepares to go to the nursing home outside Providence.

"How many books they take depend on how they're feeling. Sometimes I don't think I'm accomplishing much of anything. I had one lady who was reading real strong, but now she's slowing down."

Mrs. Riggs gathers a handful of books.

"I go from room to room and ask if they're interested. If they're sleeping or if they look real sick, I don't bother going in."

An elderly woman sits in a chair in her room. One nylon stocking is pulled above her knee. The other has fallen to her ankle. A small dish that has a picture of Jesus hangs on the wall. A walker is beside the bed.

Mrs. Riggs knocks on the open door.

"Would you like a book? I've got a romance novel that has large print."

The woman shakes her head. She says she's had a stroke.

"You might enjoy a book. Why don't you take one so you can

have something to do in the evening?"

The woman tells Mrs. Riggs she has a pretty face.

"How about 'Storm in a Rain Barrel?' It's a very good book. You don't have to give it back for two weeks."

The elderly woman says she could be dead in two weeks. But she takes the book.

Mrs. Riggs walks down the corridor, smiling at familiar faces. She sees a man watching television and pecks on his door.

"Would you care to have a book to read? I've got some nice picture stories."

The man says he doesn't read much.

"This book wouldn't be much trouble."

He looks at her but doesn't speak. After a few seconds of silence, she leaves.

A few doors down, a tiny woman holds a doll.

"May I come in? I've got some real interesting books to choose from."

The woman says she is already blind in one eye and going that way in the other. She says she used to read, but that was a long time ago.

Several of the nursing residents sit in the lobby. Some watch a talk show on the blaring television. Others doze.

Mrs. Riggs goes from chair to chair asking the same question. She gets no takers.

On her way out of the building, she sees a thin woman wearing a red, white and blue lap blanket.

"Would you care to have a book to read? I've got a whole stack."

The woman shakes her head. She says she has a Bible and doesn't read it as much as she should. She says another book would just get in the way.

The woman pulls the lap blanket tighter.

"Somebody will take one of your library books, honey," she says. "You just keep trying."

I'm in the Green Valley Road section of Newburgh, Ind., talking with a man whose residence has been reduced to little more than piles of rubble and blown insulation.

He tells a neighbor he can give him a good deal on some used bricks.

They laugh.

Another tornado victim is on top of his roof nailing sheets of paneling to plug some of the holes.

He hollers down that as a fix-it man he's in the same class as Elmer Fudd.

Those on the ground laugh.

It's 9 a.m. Sunday, only seven hours after the fickle storm sped through this Warrick County subdivision, destroying some houses and sparing others just a few feet away.

Twenty-five men, women and children died in the Tri-State. Miraculously, no one on these streets off Indiana 662 near the Vanderburgh County line was seriously hurt.

Equally amazingly, at least to me, is the coping mechanism adopted by so many folks whose homes were obliterated.

Humor.

One man stands over his van that's been crushed by a fallen tree.

He jokes that he might be able to get a few dollars for the glove compartment.

A woman surveys her mostly missing second floor and pronounces herself no longer in the market for new carpet.

I try to imagine my reaction if this was my house. If I suddenly didn't even have so much as a bathmat. If all the priceless photographs of our boys were either ruined or airborne.

First, I would be angry at my cruel fate. Of all the domiciles in the world, why did the tornado pick mine to destroy?

Then I would turn sullen. Head buried in hands. I wouldn't want to talk with anybody. Just leave me alone. Maybe I'll get over it one of these years.

I'm sure there were at least a few folks who felt this way. It's only human nature.

But everyone I approached was willing – even eager – to talk about what happened in those pre-dawn seconds.

How they found part of their master bedroom several hundred feet away in a cornfield.

How the suction of the storm was so strong they thought their eardrums would burst.

How the young couple gently explained to their little niece that she couldn't go to her room because it wasn't there any more.

Invariably, the stories ended on a high note.

While Rita Torrence's Cricklewood Street home wasn't damaged as much as some, a tree fell on her bedroom and a shard of wood shot through the wall where her pillow was.

She awakened only seconds earlier.

Was the lady anxious about where she would spend the next night?

No. She wanted to know if anyone could keep Frank, her fish, laughing that he is low-maintenance.

I wondered how she could be so upbeat at a time of such destruction.

"You're so happy to be alive that nothing else matters. You look at things differently. You aren't so serious."

The elderly woman is dying. Gurgling breaths come from congested lungs. She is covered in blankets, unable to move.

The end game is taking a long time. The flower arrangement in the hospital room that was once full is down to one drooping petal.

The daughter and son lean over on opposite sides of the bed. She kisses her mother's cheek. He wipes her brow.

The call button lights up.

The nurse at the front desk immediately rings back, asking if everything is all right.

"Sorry," the son says sheepishly.

"You set it off," the daughter says.

"Did not," the son replies.

"Did, too."

The tech comes in the room to draw blood.

"No need for that," the son says. "It just makes Mom agitated. Why can't you just let her rest in peace?"

The tech nods and walks out the door.

The small, rumpled father looks at his wife of more than five decades.

"You look good, Sweetie," he whispers in her ear.

The mother lets the air out. Her chest is silent for a few moments before heaving again.

"Remember as kids when you always made me be the Germans when we played war?" the daughter asks.

"I always had to be on the winning side," the son explains.

"Remember how you used to beat me up all the time," the daughter asks.

"Because you deserved it."

The chaplain comes in the room. The father perks up. She's been here before. He likes her.

"My Ann is a fighter," the father says proudly.

Warmed by the chaplain's bright face, the father tells her about being in the Signal Corps during the Second World War and serving in France.

"Some of the GIs didn't take the training seriously. A lot of them didn't make it."

The chaplain smiles.

My wife, MaryAnne, holds her mother's hand and remembers the woman who made the best Christmas cookies.

"My last batch at home wasn't too bad," MaryAnne says. "It wasn't like Mom's, but maybe I'm slowly getting the hang of it."

The father nudges the chaplain.

"I've got some more stories, if I'm not keeping you," Joe Stevens says.

He tells about serving at a Kentucky base before the war, and how the locals got drunk on home brew and wobbled when they walked.

Other visitors come to the room.

One plays the harp.

One wonders what is keeping Ann Stevens alive. Her organs surely shut down hours ago.

Another suggests that she is just waiting for the spirit and it hasn't come yet.

To encourage his mother to let go, Joey Stevens whispers the names of family members who have passed away.

"You can join them now. It's OK."

Ann lets the air out. Her chest is silent a little longer this time before heaving again.

The flower petal holds fast.

It will surely drop, but not yet.

I've written before about my affection for "The Andy Griffith Show," especially the episodes featuring Don Knotts as the bumbling Deputy Fife.

I think the stories were some of television's best. I also like how the small-town characters are portrayed as real people, not hapless rubes.

If I had access to a time machine, I'd park the thing outside the set of the "Griffith Show" in the early 1960s to watch a day's filming.

Alas, the conveyance was booked up, so I did the next best thing -- tracking down an actor who played a supporting rule in one of my favorite episodes.

Al Checco in "The Bank Job."

Barney becomes convinced that the Bank of Mayberry is ripe for plucking. He dresses like a cleaning woman to prove how easy it is to walk in the vault, only to have the heavy door close on him.

Frustrated that nobody is paying attention to the problem, the deputy tells two very real robbers about the lax security.

Checco, now 75, was the smaller of the would-be thieves. Black outfit. Smart-alecky. Edward G. Robinson type.

"I was called one-take Checco back then. You had to be. They shot 10 to 12 pages of script a day and there wasn't time for getting it wrong. You had to hit your mark if you wanted to be called back."

He recalls a relaxed atmosphere on the set with plenty of singing and banjo-playing between takes. Non-regulars "who had enough musical guts" joined in.

"That show had a shooting schedule different from most of the others at that time. Friday was the day set aside for everybody – not just the main characters – to read over the next week's script. The writers were there, but everybody was free to pitch lines.

"You had the weekend to think about it and filming began in earnest on Monday. The idea was to finish by Wednesday night.

The cast would get Thursday off, and then the cycle would start all over again. As I recall, I was in two or three other shows besides the episode about the bank."

Checco was one of Burgess Meredith's henchmen in TV's "Batman." The much-traveled actor also worked on "The Lucy Show" and with Phil Silvers in "Bilko."

"In those days, I was usually cast as a shady character or a kindly gentleman. My agent would hear of a role along those lines and give them my name."

Friendship helped.

"Don Knotts liked me and we worked well together. I was in a couple of his movies after he left the show. I've got his picture in my den."

A contract player in the early 1960s could count on $500 per episode. Non-stars such as Checco lived from week to week.

"Cops-and-robbers show, comedies, dramas – they all start to run together after a while. You went from one soundstage to the other."

He remembers a kindness on the "Griffith Show" that started from the top.

"Andy had a quality – I don't know how else to put it – of getting along with people. You didn't see the temper tantrums or large egos."

There was no way for Al Checco to know that "The Bank Job" would be shown hundreds of time in syndication reruns, and that the episode would become a Top 10 favorite of many veteran "Andy Griffith Show" watchers.

He was the Actors' Equity version of a Kelly Girl – report to Job Site A for three days and then head out the door in search of a paying Job Site B.

The guy still hustles work.

A Broadway play. A gig in Berlin. Voice-over commercials.

One-take Checco indeed.

"Hey, the calls still come in and I still take 'em."

He Loved Beer, Pool And Old Hank

Bobby Ray Nickens was buried Tuesday afternoon.

Hank Williams sang.

"Lord, that man of mine loved old Hank's music," says Betty Nickens, his widow. "Played it everywhere he went."

She believes her husband wouldn't want sadness and crying at his funeral.

"Bobby Ray was too full of life for that. He knew every joke in the book. Could keep you laughing 24 hours a day."

She says he would want mourners to shoot pool in his honor. And drink beer. And listen to old Hank.

Betty put a picture of Bobby Ray's motorcycle inside the casket.

And turned the volume up on some of old Hank's tunes.

"I know that 'Six More Miles to the Graveyard' was one of Bobby Ray's all-time favorites. We couldn't have a funeral without that. I thought he'd want 'Calling You' and 'Long-Gone Daddy,' so we put those on, too."

Bobby Ray was married three times. So was Betty.

"We met for the first time at a bar in Boonville (Ind.) when I was 24. I remember him telling me, 'Hey, little chicken, I want to lick your nose.' We'd see each other off and on between divorces."

He noticed the mole on his shoulder, but didn't immediately go to the doctor.

That was typical of Bobby Ray Nickens, who prided himself on being able to outwork 21-year-old guys and hated to be on the injury list for as much as a day.

The growth was eventually removed, but his health continued to deteriorate. The initial diagnosis was pneumonia. The cancer wasn't confirmed until five weeks ago.

That's when Bobby Ray asked Betty to marry him.

"He was getting pretty sick and the doctors didn't give him long to live, so we didn't wait around. The two of us went to the courthouse at Henderson, (Ky.), grabbed a couple of witnesses and had ourselves a ceremony."

When the end came, it was at his home in Tennyson, Ind.

"He went pretty fast," Betty says. "We're glad he didn't have to suffer."

Death came on June 14. He was 66.

She remembers Billy Ray shooting pool for hours at a Tennyson tavern.

And listening to old Hank.

And making sure plenty of beer was flowing.

"Nobody could handle a motorcycle better than my Bobby Ray. One time he was drinking beer in Evansville and he needed to get to Chandler (Ind.) A friend of his jumped on the back of the thing and said, 'Let's go.'

"He was thinking Bobby Ray was gonna use the road. But that's not what happened. He put that motorcycle on the railroad track and took off. It was bumpy, but they got there just fine.

"My man was wild as a buck, but in a good way. He knew people for miles and miles. It won't be the same without him."

When I pulled into the back yard of Sam Snead's Chestnut Rail Farm in Hot Springs, Va., I found one of the world's best-known golfers on top of an endloader.

"I'm a-customizin' this here gulley," he hollered down.

The man was determined to get the gulley just right. Not too much dirt in the hole. Not too much dirt on the ground.

It was 1983. I had written a letter requesting an interview. On the same piece of paper I mailed him – Slammin' Sammy was notorious for being tight with a buck – he told me to come on over.

Snead took me to his trophy room, which included a mounted Kodiak bear and numerous game fish, and yelled for his wife to bring some grapes. Snead loved grapes.

The man cussed neighborhood kids who steal his cherries. He said he's called their mamas and daddies and threatened "to switch 'em" if they try to sneak into his trees. He said his back and feet hurt "a right smart," but predicted if he ever has to quit golf, it would be because of his vision.

"I can't line up a putt worth a (expletive)."

Snead talked about playing with Presidents Eisenhower, Nixon and Ford.

An 18-hole score of 82 was good for Ike, he recalled, and that was from the short tees.

Nixon "cheated something awful," sometimes "overlooking" as many as three shots on a single hole.

Snead was in his early 70s, but had the chest and forearms of a weightlifter. He bragged that he was nimble enough during the recent harvest to avoid being injured by a runaway hay baler.
He wore his trademark straw hat during our chat. He groused that he can't keep one for more than a few weeks because people either steal the thing or poke him on top of the head with their thumbs. Even the best-made straw hat, he noted, can only stand so many thumbs.

Snead said I needed to see the restaurant he owns in Hot Springs.

I looked forward to enjoying the comfort of his shiny new Cadillac for the short ride over.

But no.

He looked at my beat-up Chevrolet Monza that barely made the three-hour trip through the mountains.

"Let's take yours," he said, climbing in the filthy front seat. "Damn gas prices are terrible."

He showed me his farm while complaining that not once has he been invited to Arnold Palmer's house. In the old days, he went on, professional golfers were all buddies.

"Now there's no socializin' whatsoever."

Only a handful of customers were inside the restaurant, which brought on another round of expletives.

Snead snorted that they only send him bills, never profits.

The man asked out loud if anybody wanted to buy the place. Several diners reached for pens, but for autographs -- not offer sheets.

"Just kidding, y'all."

On our way back to the farm, Snead told me about a recent visit to South Africa when he got into a dispute with an ostrich that picked up his ball and galloped to the next fairway. He hit the thing in the face, and said the resulting hand injury kept him out of three tournaments.

I laughed, something that I did many times during our 90 minutes together. Sam Snead was old-school, unpretentious and home-spun – pretty good qualities for a guy recognized around the globe, but was happiest at home in Western Virginia.

He died last week at his beloved Hot Springs.

I'll bet there's a lot more socializin' in heaven.

Sometimes Rick Smithhart turns his house into a bunker. He blocks out all light, establishes a perimeter and walks point.

The 55-year-old Evansville man says he rarely sleeps more than two hours a night, and often wakes up to sweat-soaked nightmares about having to identify stacks of blood-drenched troops.

When a car backfires, he dives to the floor and covers his head.

Smithhart was a Marine in Vietnam in the late 1960s. He says more than 80 percent of his unit was either killed or wounded. He escaped with shrapnel holes throughout his body.

"We were known as the walking dead. Every night we listened to Hanoi Hannah on the radio. 'Today, you walk, Marine. Tonight, you die.' I thought it was pretty amusing."

The discharge papers say Smithhart mustered out of the service in 1971.

But the burly man is still in Southeast Asia.

And he may never be able to leave.

"I felt comfortable in Vietnam. It was simple. They were trying to kill us and we were trying to kill them. I'll never be as good at anything as I was in combat."

When civilians spit on him at airports, his fists flew as instinctively as setting his rifle on automatic during ambushes. The MPs learned to keep an eye on him.

Smithhart is in counseling for post-traumatic stress disorder. He has three failed marriages. He has been treated for alcohol abuse. He has difficulty holding jobs.

"For me, the perfect day would be to have a fishing pole in the water, a campfire going and to be left alone."

This afternoon he is at the VFW Post on Wabash Avenue.

"Some of these people had similar military experiences to mine. I can relax with them."

Smithhart shows that trust by allowing some members to sit behind him.

"If I was elsewhere, I'd have to face the rest of the room. I'd be edgy the whole time like something bad was gonna happen."

One of his last assignments in Vietnam was to identify dead bodies before they were shipped back to the United States.

"There was a whole warehouse full of mutilated corpses. Some of the men were still holding their weapons and I had to pry them out of their fingers. Every so often I'd stop what I was doing so they could hose down the blood."

The other men in the room nurse drinks and watch television. Rick Smithhart is not at ease. His eyes dart back and forth like he's still on duty.

"I would be a very successful businessman today if I hadn't gone to Vietnam. I have not resolved anywhere near my every potential. But I accept it. There's nothing I can do to change it."

Serving his nation, Smithhart says, was a good thing.

"I had a tremendous amount of patriotism. I never felt like the government owes me anything."

Vietnam, he believes, became a mistake.

"The war got political. We would take a position and give it back. I questioned some of the strategy and it got me in trouble."

If you were a younger man, I wondered, would you volunteer to fight in Iraq?

"I would go right now as a 55-year-old. It's what I do."

Last week's mine tragedy in West Virginia prompted memories of death down under when I lived in Appalachia.

I recalled the stories told me by wheezing old men who survived explosions in deep mines when they were young bucks, and couldn't breathe without spitting up coal dust.

They talked about bodies that had been tossed around like kernels in a popcorn popper. And about the swollen, blue faces of the dead. And about the delay in having proper funerals because the rural funeral homes weren't equipped to handle so many corpses.

I sat next to family members as they waited in churches and school cafeterias for news of loved ones trapped hundreds of feet underground.

They told me about praying that their daddy would come out of the shaft only missing an arm or a leg or a few fingers.

And how if their daddy is among the dead, they'll pay money they don't have for the nicest tombstone in the undertaker's collection. Gotta put 'em away right, they said.

The mine disaster I remember best took place in Topmost, Ky., in December of 1981. Eight men were killed.

They didn't suffer, as death set in before they could reach for self-rescuer devices. Their clothes were burned from their bodies.

Robert Slone, 39, was among the departed. A few days after the funeral, his wife Ora gave birth to their eighth child.

The woman had a bad feeling about the Potato Creek mine. She kept dreaming that she was in a graveyard, picking twigs and leaves off the markers.

Robert didn't like talking about his job. All she knew was that he worked in a small mine with a 40-inch top, and that his back ached every second he was underground, and that it sometimes took him an hour to thoroughly straighten up after a shift.

Around Thanksgiving, one of the children asked what he was getting Ora for Christmas.

Robert Slone pointed to his wife's big belly, and said what was in there would be the best present of them all.

Ora was preparing an afternoon snack for the kids when a sudden explosion rattled the windows. She knew it was bad. There had been previous jolts from inside the mine, but none with this much concussion.

The lady expected the worst and that's what happened.

The doctor was afraid the trauma of identifying the body might cause Ora to lose the baby. So the task went to her 20-year-old daughter, Josephine.

The young woman couldn't bear to look at her father's face. She could tell by Robert's pudgy fingers and his new wristwatch that the toe tag on the body had the right name.

Josephine was proud to be the first in the family to go to college. In teasing fashion, Robert referred to her as "his favorite little accountant," even though he knew Josephine was studying to be a teacher.

The young woman said Robert didn't want any of his sons to work underground. He hoped he would be the last coal miner in his household.

I talked with Ora Slone a few years after the explosion. She said Robert left a $50,00 insurance policy. A good chunk of the money went to a new house with electric heat.

Ora told me her husband "never lived for even one minute" in such a cozy place.

"He would have really like this."

She paused to find the right words.

"We never could while he was living. He had to die first."

I give you Roger Cox, who just might be the best demolition derby driver in Western civilization.

You can look up the stats.

Derbies entered: 480. Derbies won: 407.

Or you can just ask him.

"When the other guys see me arrive in the infield, they know the only smart thing to do is put their cars back on the flatbeds and go home."

The man holds forth from a 60-acre junkyard he owns outside Evansville. Mud, fenders, piles of beer cans – this place has it all.

"If you're gonna derby, you gotta win. Only way you can afford to keep entering. You can get a $25 car, last maybe two minutes, have a little fun and lose. Or you can be like me and go in prepared to come out first."

Which means spending up to $500 for a GM station wagon from the mid 1970s. And investing almost that much on a good transmission. And spending hour after greasy hour transferring parts from dead cars to the one you're going to play bumper pool in on Saturday night.

"I figure a derby car on time. Will it beat and bang for 10 minutes, or will it go for two hours? That's what I do best, even better than driving. I know how to fix a car to last the two hours.

"Can't use a Cadillac. Run it a few minutes and the pressure cap flies off the radiator. Can't use any car with a big motor. They get hot and they won't let you go backwards more than a little while without blowing. The car you really want is a '98 Olds, but try finding one.

"Another thing I'm big on is knowing exactly what the rules are at a particular derby. Can you low-gear the rear end? Will they let you put water in the tires? Can you weld the frames? You find out what's legal, and then you go to work on the car."

Gee, Roger, aren't demo derbies just a simple way for rednecks with motor oil in their veins to have a little fun?

"Probably was that way 20 years ago when half the drivers were drunk. Now you've got professionals behind the wheel. They'll come from 800 miles away if you give 'em a shot at a good pay day."

Which would be how much?

"Usually it's $1,000 to the overall winner, but I've made $15,000."

Let's talk strategy.

"Go after the other guy's front end. Pop a tie rod or hit the drag link so it won't steer.

And don't jump out to the middle right off the bat. Let the crazies do that and knock themselves out. Then go after the sane ones."

Ever been hurt?

"Nothing serious. Just some busted ribs, and I've been scalded pretty good when the antifreeze in the car beside me spewed out. I tell 'em to use plain water and that won't happen."

Ever been in a fight, Roger? Don't take this the wrong way, but you do come across a little, well, cocky.

"Been fussed at a time or two, but it never came to fists. They're afraid of me."

What do you see as the future for demolition derbies?

"Ain't no future. Can't find the '70s model cars that you need. No sense wasting your time going to the derby with something made in the '80s or '90s. They accordion up to almost nothing. And they got front-wheel drive and that's worthless on a derby car."

Gee, Roger, you sound downright bummed out.

"The days that I go through 50 derby cars a year are gone. Might promote some derbies. Might run in a few just so they'll know who the man is. But the truth is, I'm trying to quit."

August 12, 1990
A Duty To Hit The Right Gravesite Notes

FAIRFIELD, Ill. – Myrl Newcom begged the Army to take him during the Second World War, going so for as to take the physical three times.

Heart murmur, the doctors diagnosed. Won't keep me from shooting straight, Newcom argued. Forget it, they said.

So he went to college and later took a job at the war plant in Herrin, Ill.

"I felt bad that I wasn't able to fight. I had a guilt complex a mile wide. Men were getting shot up overseas and there I was, going home every day when my shift was over."

Newcom majored in music education at the University of Illinois and Southern Illinois University. He taught band and chorus at both the high school and grade school levels.

For fun, the 72-year-old Wayne County man plays the trumpet for concert bands.

For duty, he blows taps at military funerals.

He started the cemetery gig in 1946, and continues to play the sorrowful notes when called upon, either by funeral homes or the families of deceased ex-servicemen. Some folks in Fairfield believe he should have a seat of honor on the podium when the town celebrates Veterans Day.

"I never turn anyone down when asked to play. They don't even have to thank me."

Newcom reckons he's played taps at more than 200 funerals, sometimes as often as three times a week.

"About half the time I know the man I'm playing for. But I do them all. I'm there when an 85-year-old man dies of old age, and I'm there when a Vietnam veteran commits suicide."

Newcom stands alone at the cemetery, his cornet tucked under his arm. He watches the honor guard remove the flag from the coffin. He watches the 21-gun salute. When the smoke clears, he plays a two-minute version of the tune. The service is over when he puts down the instrument.

"Sometimes people will want to tip me 20 bucks or even 40. I always say no. Since I didn't serve, playing at the funeral is the least I can do for those who did."

He says he uses a cornet "because most bugles are made cheap and they don't sound good."

Newcom never gets emotional.

"Even if it's someone I knew well, I'm busy concentrating on the music. I've never had a problem with crying or anything like that."

Once he was fishing when the call came.

"I stuck the pole in the bank and went to the house to put my tie and jacket on. I played the funeral and then I went back to the lake and picked up where I left off."

Does he consider himself a dying tradition?

"I hope not. I hope our country never gets to the point where a musician won't play at a military funeral if asked. You should want to play, even if it isn't convenient."

Myrl Newcom says he won't let age cancel a gravesite performance.

"I'll be doing it when I'm 80 and I hope I'll be doing it if I get to 100. I play as well as when I was younger, so there's no reason not so. I owe the guys who served their country and I'll keep owing them."

No Purple Hearts For Bullet-Riddled Buddy

"Hey, Garret, who's your buddy in the front seat? Doesn't look human."

He's not, thanks for asking. He's a silhouette target for the military. Stands about three feet, six inches. Name is Half Soldier.

"Looks all shot up."

He is. That's what happens when troops fire at you.

"Odd choice of a traveling companion, wouldn't you say?"

Not at all. Some people go to Disneyland when they have a few days off. I go to Army bases. Actually, not all Army bases. Just the one where I trained.

"Where might that be, Garret?"

Fort Leonard Wood in Missouri, perhaps the most God-forsaken place in the universe that doesn't have abandoned lunar rovers.

"So Half Soldier is a souvenir."

Exactly.

"Did you buy the thing at the PX?"

Nope. Got him at the firing range.

"Say what?"

Half Soldier was in a trash can. I guess you could say I liberated him.

"What were you doing at the firing range?"

In the early fall of 1971, some decidedly unpleasant persons marched me out there during basic training.

"You mean drill sergeants?"

Exactly. I had enough anxiety to fuel an aircraft carrier. I sincerely believed they were going to kill me.

"So you decided to return to the scene of the near crime."

That's right. I wanted to stand in the Missouri prairie and reminisce without being shouted at by decidedly unpleasant persons.

"Were you a good soldier?"

No. I was particularly woeful at folding my underwear and making my bed, things the Pentagon considered every bit as important as taking out enemy fire bases.

"*Could you shoot the M16?*"

As a rifleman, I ranked with the invertebrates. I was to pouring lead as Barney Fife was to Audie Murphy.

"*So when the Army mounted a silhouette target for you to aim at, the thing stood an excellent change of remaining in pristine condition after you emptied your weapon?*"

Exactly.

"*And for this deficiency, you caught much grief?*"

Yes. The decidedly unpleasant persons became almost certifiable if a half-wit of a basic trainee couldn't hit the stupid target.

"*So what happened at the firing range on your visit to Fort Leonard Wood?*"

I was strolling around the grounds, recalling the embarrassing afternoon when I temporarily misplaced the bolt assembly and the captain threatened to drop-kick my hind parts all the way to St. Louis.

"*Were you alone?*"

Just me and Half Soldier.

"*So you stole him?*"

I prefer to think of my buddy as a symbol of man's unceasing struggle to prevail.

"*What do you mean?*"

In the end, I was the ultimate winner. While I couldn't shoot Half Soldier, I was more than capable of taking him home.

"*Won't keep you, Garret. Know that you and your thin friend have a lot to talk about.*"

Thanks for understanding. We're going out for drinks.

"*What kind?*"

Shooters.

October 29, 2000
Death Motivates Drifter To Change Life

Oct. 19. 11 p.m. A CSX train roared through Henderson, Ky. Randy Hall, 38, sat on the tracks. He'd been drinking.

The locomotive can't stop in time and Hall is thrown 40 feet into the weeds. He is pronounced dead at the scene.

His cousin, James Huff, was a few feet away and escaped injury. He also had been drinking.

Huff spent the night in jail. He was fined $164 and charged with trespassing.

Hall's body was cremated.

The two men were drifters. They spent several days at the Rescue Mission in Evansville before hitchhiking to Henderson the afternoon of the accident.

"That night changed my life," Huff says, crying. "I lost my best friend in the world. My eyes have been opened. I'm through with the beer."

The pals lived most of their lives in Cleveland. Huff worked on machinery and his friend painted houses.

"We had to get away from the city. Crime. Drugs all over the place. Terrible place to live. Randy's 12-year-old son lives in Tucson (Ariz.). We were there two years ago and loved the climate. He was crazy about that boy. That's where we were going when the train…"

He stops to compose himself.

"We'd work a few days. Get paid. Get a bus ticket. Move a little further down the road. Stay in a motel if we had the money. Stay in a mission if we didn't.

"We weren't bums. Traveling men, there's a difference. We kept ourselves clean. We didn't mess with anybody."

I point out that he hasn't mentioned anything about the drinking.

"That was part of it. I'm not gonna lie. I didn't do it too bad unless something was bothering me and I was going through a bad time. I didn't drink to get drunk.

"But Randy did. Thinking about his son was killing him inside. He'd put down a 12-pack and then start in on the wine."

I ask the man to go back to Oct. 19.

"Randy wanted to leave the Rescue Mission even though we had a good job unloading trucks. I didn't want him to go alone, so I went along. We heard there was work across the river in Henderson, so that's where we headed.

"I had $18 and used some of it to buy beer. We didn't want to get caught drinking on the street, so we went to the railroad tracks. It's thick with trees and nobody would know we were there.

"I had four or five cans and fell asleep on this flat place down the slope from the tracks. I didn't hear the train. I didn't find out what happened until I asked the police where Randy was and they told me he didn't make it."

He starts to cry again.

"Earlier that night, Randy did something he had never done before. He asked me to pray with him over Jeremy. He was really hurting. You know somebody like I knew Randy and you can tell."

Huff says he likes Henderson and would like to live there.

I ask how much money he has.

"Nothing, but I'll work. I've always worked."

Hall's family in Cleveland has asked for the papers he was carrying when he died.

"I've been going around to the churches of Henderson trying to get money for a bus ticket. If I can't get any help, I'll hitchhike. That's what his people want and that's what I'll do. I'd go to the ends of the Earth for that boy."

As a former summer replacement garbageman who once worked four straight days without hurling until I emptied the contents of a rodent colony, I must protest the automatic thingie used these days to hoist rubbish containers.

If a modern-day garbage process-server comes across a receptacle that is too heavy, or too smelly, or too laden with gnawing mammals, he can affix it to a device on the back of the truck that catapults the stuff into the hopper.

He doesn't hoist the can.

He doesn't have a personal relationship with the slop inside the can.

He simply activates the automatic thingie and hydraulics takes care of the rest.

No muss, no fuss, no peristalsis.

He probably doesn't even wear gloves.

This does a tremendous disservice to those of us who came this way before.

Those of us who not only wore gloves, but scrubbed our hands in 20 Mule Team Borax so our fingers wouldn't rot off and give females yet another reason to go to the dance with somebody else.

I only hope that the men who handle rotted foodstuffs on today's trash trucks have the good grace not to call themselves "garbagemen."

That's our word.

They are "automatic thingiemen."

Big difference.

To be a garbageman is to lift.

Doesn't matter if the can is 99 percent cinderblocks with only a dollop of trash on top to satisfy the legal requirement.

You lift.

Doesn't matter if the can is filled with homemade pickles so foul that maggots took one taste and staged an emergency evacuation.

You lift.

We started early and worked late, usually because the truck mysteriously stopped running in the heat of the afternoon.

Our driver, a wise fellow who knew there had to be some perks to the job beyond the $1.75 an hour and shirts with your name on them, made sure the breakdown occurred near a beer store.

To be a garbageman is to learn to stand downwind.

Proper – and even improper society – does not want to mingle with persons who see the basic food groups at their absolute worst.

Automatic thingiemen can eat with the queen.

We dined around the grease rack.

To be a garbageman is to never – and I mean never – return the lid of a trash can to its rightful place.

That would violate the only rule of the job.

Do not touch something nasty more than once.

The way we flung the tops, I wouldn't be surprised if some ended up in outer space.

Orbiting trash can covers.

Courtesy of your handy-dandy garbageman.

It is the proudest of legacies.

PRINCETON, Ky. – The other day, a preliminary hearing was held in Caldwell County District Court for accused bootlegger, Birdie Lee Smith.

She was cited by police following a raid at her house in which 139 cans of beer, 42 half-pints of liquor and $164.91 was confiscated.

Caldwell County is dry, meaning alcohol sales are prohibited.

Birdie Lee is 91 years old.

I talked with a prominent Princeton man who has known her for more than 40 years. He admitted buying beer from the lady when he was in high school, saying it was almost a rite of passage.

He said she helped raise several children whose parents either abandoned them or lacked the resources to provide proper care. He said she has been arrested for bootlegging more times than anybody can count.

The man told me it's impossible to get mad at Birdie Lee because she is always smiling. When she comes to court, it's like a reunion. She greets lawmen, court officials and attorneys as if they are life-long friends.

Nobody has the heart to put her in jail. She happily pays the fine, waves goodbye and goes back to where she came from.

I talked with Birdie Lee Smith after the court appearance.

"The bootlegging, well, it's something that I work at a while and then quit for a while. Most times I send runners to Hopkinsville (Ky.) to get it. Sometimes they cheat me, charge for something and steal it. They know I'm old so they misuse me.

"I don't drive any more 'cause I can't see good enough. I don't walk too much either 'cause my head starts swimming. I've got lots of friends. They know I'm an old widow woman, so they come up on the hill and look out for me.

"I like to go to the race track with $100 and bet on the horses. If I say I want to go to Ellis Park, I don't have any trouble at all getting a ride. If a holiday comes up, I've always got plenty of people who come see me.

"Truth is the light. If I tell you something, it's not gonna be a double-cross. We have fun when I go to court. I tell 'em things like 'I'm sweet 16' or 'Mama's got to get back home now.' They know I'm not out to hurt anybody. When they say they have a search warrant, I tell 'em to help themselves.

"No indeedy, I'm not a drinker. If I was a drinker, how could I sell it? Some people who do what I do get called out of bed at 3 o'clock in the morning to make a sale. That doesn't happen to Mama 'cause they respect me too much. They wait until a proper time of day.

"I've got maybe 50 customers, people I know real good. Payday people, I call 'em. I'll sell a half-pint for $3 unless I have to go too far to get it. Money's scarce. You've got to hit and run.

"I'm not a rich person. Who told you that? A lot of the money I get goes to help the kids I've taken in. Did you know that I've even sent some to college? Do I have any regrets? Yeah, I wish I had children of my own. Other than that, I'm happy. I know I'm going to heaven. I'm only here until the good Lord takes me.

"I keep a quiet place. No fighting. They don't even arrest me. They just tell me to go to court and post bond. I do what they say. I don't want to make a fuss."

Does this arrest mean the end of your bootlegging career?"

Big grin.

"If I catch a bargain, well, you never know. If someone wants to know where they can get something, I might help out. It can't be a regular thing, though. I'm an old woman."

Lawman Recalls The Case Of The Skunk

ENFIELD, Ill. – It's the rare police investigation, village officer Mike Lydick notes, that makes a lawman laugh so hard he can't stand up.

"In a small town like Enfield (population 900), you have to be a combination psychologist, preacher and cop – depending on what's necessary at the time," says the 46-year-old Lydick. "When I'm working a case, I don't expect to crack up."

But that's exactly what happened two weeks ago.

"I thought they'd have to call an ambulance for me. There for a while I actually couldn't get my breath. It was impossible for me to have the composure you expect a policeman to have."

It began with a telephone call from a resident of an apartment complex in town.

"There was a complaint about a skunk inside one of the units. I followed the smell and knocked on the door. The woman said, 'It's not the skunk, it's me.' Then she said she took a bath in tomato juice, but the odor wouldn't come out. It was very apparent that she had been drinking heavily.

"I was acquainted with her from another police matter. When she's not drinking, she's as kind as can be. But, bless her heart, with the bottle, she's like Jekyll and Hyde.

"She's an animal lover. I'm not sure whether she hit the skunk with her car or if she picked it up by the side of the road. I don't even know if the skunk was dead or alive. I do know that she took it back to her apartment.

"I didn't get past the stairs. I couldn't. It smelled like the skunk was right at my feet. Going in the apartment would have been more than I could stand."

So there was no thorough investigation of the crime scene?

"That's right. I got out of that doorway as fast as I could and started to laugh myself silly."

And you failed to conduct a comprehensive interview with the suspect?

"A policeman can't make sense with someone when he's got tears coming down his face."

And there was no autopsy of the skunk to determine cause of death?

"That's right."

Lydick, the lone lawman in this White County community, later learned that the woman went to at least one Enfield business after her close encounter with the animal, and that her visit resulted in a huge run on Lysol.

"There aren't any statutes on the books for having a skunk in your apartment. I looked at it as more of an animal control problem than a violation of the law."

Have you seen the woman since the incident?

"No, but I'm sure she feels bad about what happened and wants to put it behind her."

Tell us another story about enforcing the law in Enfield.

"These two guys went through town at 1 o'clock in the morning going 20 miles per hour over the speed limit. It was in January and the wind chill was about 10 below. When I got up to the car, I noticed that they didn't have anything on but T-shirts and jeans.

"You could have cut the marijuana smoke with a knife. I had them get out of the car while I conducted a search. They were shivering inside of two minutes. One said, 'Look, man, that's my pot and that's my beer. We're guilty. Put us in that warm police car.' Which I did. They turned out to be the nicest young men you could meet. Neither had any prior arrests. They just happened to have that one day when they cut loose a little too much and happened to get caught. Seeing them with blue toes made me laugh."

But not like the time with the skunk.

"No. That was a classic."

April 24, 1994
Max The Dog Deals With Loss Of Best Friend

ELBERFELD, Ind – Max, the combination terrier-beagle, will be 5 years old next month. He lives at the Menke house on Fifth Street near the elementary school.

The dog went through a period of depression last month, but now is beginning to show signs of his former self. He's putting on weight, barks less and responds with a wag of the tail when someone plays with his ears.

"Max is spoiled," said Margaret Menke. "But it's our fault. We pretty much let him do anything he wants. There's supposed to be a rule that he stays out of the living room, but he'll give us one of those looks and, well, you know."

The 65-year-old Warrick County woman married Vernon Menke, her high school sweetheart, in 1948.

Menke, a big man who liked to laugh, owned a garage where he repaired farm equipment. He also worked for 23 years in the coal mines.

"It must have been tough to go to the mine after he'd been working on tractors all day, but Vernon never complained. He'd rather work than sit."

Max was supposed to be a present for one of the grandchildren. Things didn't work out, and Vernon was asked if he would assume custody.

"He didn't want the dog at first," Margaret said. "He'd get all grumpy and go on and on about how he was too old to take care of a chubby little dog."

But Max grew on him.

"I think they got close because Max is such a showoff. The dog will limp to get sympathy and then forget which leg is supposed to be hurting. When he gets hungry, he'll start wagging his tail and then get real disappointed if you don't immediately give him something to eat."

If Vernon crawled under a tractor, Max crawled under a tractor. If Vernon went to town, Max went to town.

"Vernon had this 1946-model Jeep that he used to run errands. Max got in the habit of riding on the hood. Vernon would have let him sit on the seat, but I guess the dog didn't get enough wind that way. Everybody knew Vernon was coming because they could see his big hood ornament. Not once did Max fall off."

The two were inseparable companions. Vernon took him to the fire hall where he was a volunteer firefighter. He took the pet to the field when he checked on his cows.

"The way they got along beat anything you've ever seen," Margaret said. "We practically had to chain the dog up so he wouldn't follow Vernon to the coal mine."

Vernon retired in 1993 and used the time to go fishing. Max was always at his feet.

"On March 25, Vernon was watching a basketball game on television," Margaret said. "Vernon looked like he was about to doze off, so I went to bed and left the light on for him. I had no idea anything was wrong.

"I woke up a few hours later and went to check on him. He was sitting just like he was when I left him, but he wasn't breathing. His heart just stopped."

More than 1,500 people signed the book at the funeral home. Services had to be delayed until everyone could find a seat.

"Everybody liked Vernon," Margaret said. "You couldn't help it."

Max wasn't the same. He wouldn't eat. He didn't respond when family members played with his ears.

"It's like they say – dogs can tell when something is wrong. We tried everything to cheer him up, but Max was as sad as he could be.

"The boys came up with the idea the day of the visitation. They asked the undertaker if it would be all right if Max saw Vernon one last time. So on Sunday night at 9 o'clock after all the people left, they brought Max to the funeral home. They held him up so he could look into the casket. He licked Vernon's hand and put his nose on his face.

"That made all the difference in the world. The next day Max started to show more energy. It was as if he understood what happened."

ELDERLY GENTLEMAN WISHES TO MEET ELDERLY LADY. GOOD CHARACTER IN 80S. BILL.

ROBINSON, Ill. – This classified advertisement – with address information included – was placed in newspapers in Crawford and Lawrence counties earlier this month by a 91-year-old fellow named Bill McClure.

He means what he says.

"I don't have any use for a woman less than 80. I've had four ladies get in touch with me since the ad came out, but none of 'em are old enough. Shoot, one gal was only 63."

McClure, who worked as a roofer until he was 82, doesn't think a serious relationship can develop unless the female approaches his age. In other words, he doesn't want to talk World War 1 and have his companion for the evening say, "Huh?"

"I know some women around here I could live with right now – you know, not get married – but that would be wrong. I'm the type of man who wants to do things the good way."

He married Alta in 1916 and they had four children. She died three years ago and he lives alone in a small apartment on the second floor above the Goodwill store.

A bare bulb dangles from the hall ceiling. The floor creaks. The walls could use a scrubbing. Dust coats the steep stairs.

"I never imagined I'd ever think about another woman again, what with Alta and me being married so long. I sold almost all the furniture we had and got ready to bach it for the rest of my life.

"Then a few months ago, I started feeling lonely. My kids don't like to write letters, and I found myself with not much to do to fill the day. I got to thinking about maybe being able to find a reasonable enough woman to get married to. That's when I put the ads in the papers."

On the one hand, Bill McClure would seem a first-rate catch. He walks, does exercises and drives his 1982 Dodge wherever he wants to go. He doesn't smoke, drink or cuss.

But the guy does have shortcomings. He admits to being a loner who likes to spend long hours looking for mushrooms. He gets bored with women who want to play cards all the time, and who can't talk about anything more substantial than what went on at the Eagles Club on Saturday night.

The woman he selects would have to agree to let him live in her house following the "very private" wedding.

"I don't think that's asking too much. I believe in treating a woman right. I'm willing to give 60 percent and only take 40."

McClure knew he would marry Alta after their second date.

"We had our disagreements over the years, but I know now that she was right at least nine out of every 10 times. I ended up eating a lot of crow."

He plans to meet – and evaluate – every "elderly lady" who responds to his ad.

"There are a lot of widow women in Robinson. I might end up marrying one of 'em and then maybe I won't. I know one thing. It won't be anything I'll pine away about."

His progress so far?

"There hasn't been a woman even close. They're too young, or they smoke, or they live with their children. I tell 'em the truth straight out and then I move on. A man my age doesn't want to waste his time."

BONE GAP, Ill. – Brown folding chairs line the floor of the old gymnasium that was built back when the blueprints for a barn and a place to play basketball were almost interchangeable.

Most of the folks who sit in the folding chairs have white hair and wrinkled faces.

Many of the men have freshly starched white shirts and scrubbed black shoes. Many of the women wear homespun dresses and carry big, black handbags.

The band strikes up an Ernest Tubb tune. The senior citizens tap their feet and drum their fingers on the chairs. Men tap their lady friends on the shoulder and point the way to mid-court.

The partners smile as they put each other through the paces – the two-step, the waltz, the jig. There's an occasional dip and, once in a great while, a pirouette.

But mostly they just hold each other.

This is their night.

This is their music.

In a world that caters more and more to the young and trendy, the weekly Bone Gap Opry is a throwback to a simpler time.

The singers and musicians perform without pay and take the small stage in the order they arrived. When everyone has had a turn, master of ceremonies Charlie Moore goes back to the first sign-up on his rumpled list and it starts again.

There are no prima donnas at the Bone Gap Opry. If your star is too bright to hang your coat on a nail in back of the stage, best not come to this corner of Edwards County. If your guitar case is too good to lean against a radiator, best take it elsewhere.

The Bone Gap School is the host. The Bone Gap Ruritan Club is the sponsor. There's no admission fee, no ticket, nobody to stamp your hand as you go in. A donation box was good enough generations ago when the boiler was installed and it's good enough now.

When the Opry wants pageantry, it puts on a contest for Valentine Sweetheart. When it wants excitement, it raffles off two tickets for a ham-and-bean supper. When it wants humor, Moore tells a chicken-crossing-the-road joke.

Sisters dance with sisters and grandfathers dance with grand-daughters. Sometimes they are in time to the music and sometimes they aren't. That's all right. There is no rhythm committee at the Bone Gap Opry, no final arbiters of form and style.

The band plays "Rolling in My Sweet Baby's Arms." Dance floor participation is almost 100 percent. Some of the starched shirts have worked themselves free of their belts. Drops of sweat dribble down necks that are pressed against the collars of the homespun dresses.

The smell of popcorn gives the musty smell of the gymnasium a run for its money. A man on stage says he wishes he could sing better, but he just can't.

Hearts are filled with contentment, souls with serenity. For this moment, at least, all is right with the world.

And they dance.

Donald Kaiser lives alone in a public housing apartment building that's as small as it is spartan.

Bed. Refrigerator. TV set. End table. Wobbly chair. Notes to himself written on crumpled envelopes.

Nothing to suggest the Evansville man fought in three wars and almost got his nose blown off.

That would be showy, and that's something Donald Kaiser isn't. The stories about the fighting don't come unless you ask, and even then they're only a trickle.

His war medals are on the table. He only talks about them in summary form, saying he had jobs to do the three times he went overseas and always tried to do his best.

"Don't have much money," the 81-year-old man says. "I'm on 30 percent disability. I'm trying to get the government to move that up some. About all I have that's extra are these things."

He points to several dozen cigars in a neat stack.

"I go through about 20 a day. Been smoking 'em since I was a kid."

Donald doesn't get out much. The VFW lodge. The barber shop. The beer joint down the street.

There's no car. If he needs to go somewhere, he takes the bus and tries to remember his cane. He's fallen more than once, and his daughter gets on his case for not being more careful.

The quiet-spoken man shows me a booklet that Veterans Affairs gave him about post-traumatic stress disorder.

"That's what I have. I get nightmares. Sometimes I hear a loud noise or a siren and I think I'm back in the war."

A kitchen cabinet is full of pills to calm him down and lower his blood pressure.

"When I got home from Korea, I had to have a shotgun by my side and pistol under my bed before I felt safe. My wife didn't like that and we ended up getting a divorce."

He served in the Philippines during the Second World War.

"We're in our foxholes and the Japanese are hollering out, 'Hey, Joe.' They wanted you to answer so they could shoot you down."

Donald was shot in the leg in 1951 during the Korean War. The doctors couldn't remove all the shrapnel.

"It felt hot when it happened, like a real bad sting."

In 1967, during his second tour in Vietnam, he was shot in the face.

"I was a bloody mess and my nose was just hanging. The doctor said he'd put it back as good as he could. I think he did all right."

He got jobs in law enforcement after coming back from Southeast Asia, but the PTSD got worse.

"I thought it would be better if I just stopped working."

They call him "Sarge" around the apartment building. He likes that.

Donald Kaiser put off filing for the six medals he earned for his service in Korea.

A service officer with the VA helped with the paperwork and the long-overdue medals arrived earlier this year. There was a ceremony the other day at the VFW.

"A lieutenant colonel saluted me. That was something. I got called a veteran's veteran. It was a good day."

Few men, I point out, fought in three wars and lived to tell about it.

"The Army was good to me, and I guess I was good for the Army."

June 5, 1990
Window-Washer Cleans Up After Tornado

PETERSBURG, Ind. – On Monday, two days after the tornado, there was noise.

Power saws slicing fallen trees into manageable lengths. Bulldozers scraping the remains of houses and garages from rutted yards. Helicopters feinting and jabbing the clouds with rescue supplies in tow.

All loud.

All what you'd expect in the wake of devastating tornadoes that claimed four lives in this Pike County town and destroyed more than 100 homes. Cleaning up after one of the worst natural disasters in Indiana history isn't hush-hush work.

Rick Cobb's noise was harder to hear.

The 43-year-old Cobb, a self-admitted goofy guy, operates a window-cleaning business out of his Monroe City, Ind., home. It's a one-person operation unless you count his 11-year-old daughter, Brooke, who occasionally tags along.

His noise?

The squish-squishing of squeegee against storefront glass made rickety by Saturday's storms.

"You can just barely touch the windows and feel them shake."

Cobb spent the day washing windows in downtown Petersburg. The tavern. The bank. The insurance agency. The baseball card shop. Charged no fee. Left no business cards.

"Washing windows is my way of making people feel better. Maybe they'll see what I'm doing and their morale will be raised. I guess it's a kind of therapy."

He said he had 45 window-washing clients in Petersburg, mostly offices.

"That was before Saturday, though. At least half those businesses were either destroyed or damaged. A lot of people will take whatever insurance money they can get and pull out. I feel for them. It's a real shame."

Cobb didn't check his ledger to see if a storefront belonged to a client. He walked up and down Main Street -- lugging a five-gallon bucket of solvent -- and washed them all. He ran out of water at noon and went home to get a fresh supply.

"It's a sin if you see a chance to help and ignore it."

He came to Petersburg Saturday night after he heard about the tornado on his police scanner.

"I've had some EMT training and thought they could use somebody like that. Power lines were down all over the road. I couldn't get any closer than four miles from town, so I parked the car and walked."

He stayed until early Sunday, concentrating his efforts at the Petersburg Health Care Center where his father-in-law, Robert Schuckman, is a patient.

"I hadn't gotten much sleep, so my appearance probably wasn't too good. The police thought I might get mistaken for a burglar. I showed them the logo on the back of my parka ("Your Pane Is Our Pleasure"). I said it glows in the dark so they'd be sure to know where to mail my body. That must've been a pretty good response because I didn't have any more trouble."

Cobb is one of the few window-washers in this part of the country who uses words like "vibes" and "karma." He said he graduated from Indiana University with a degree in business administration, "but I never learned anything in school that applies to the real world. On the whole, I'd rather wear jeans and wash windows."

He started cleaning the front glass on Anderson's Heating and Air Conditioning that was pounded into submission by the twister.

J.C. Anderson, the owner of the business, watches the squeegee go up and down.

"How come you're washing my windows?" he asks.

"To keep in practice," Cobb replies. "This is how I get my kicks. You don't mind, do you?"

Anderson smiles.

Rick Cobb's therapy was already working.

Dear Sierria,

First of all, let me say how much I enjoy taking you and the other fourth-grade children out for a few hours after school.

The mall, the museum, the playground, the baseball game – you kids vote and I become the wheelman.

I miss having young folks around the house.

Fatherhood is the most wonderful thing of all. But when it's over, it's over. There's nothing left except the baby cheetah poster on the wall, and the petrified remains of a Hershey bar under the bed from a long-ago sleepover.

You girls and boys help me keep those memories alive.

Thanks.

There's something else, too.

Many of you have it rough away from school. Your caregivers struggle to make ends meet. You learn to do without.

Our time together provides experiences you might otherwise not have.

Watching your faces light up gives me a glow that lasts for days.

Many of you live in places where there are too many shady characters. Too many police sirens.

Our time together is a respite from that environment.

We talk about the importance of reading and writing. My dream is that some of you can use education to catapult out of your difficult circumstances.

Your path, Sierria, will be decidedly uphill.

Money is tight. The family has no car. Mom and Dad are on fixed incomes. There are health issues.

But you are resilient.

And dogged.

I've never seen a child go about a task with such a sense of purpose.

You know the tale about the tortoise and the hare?

Just keep going, little girl. You'll come out ahead in the end.

Something you did the other day, Sierria, almost made me cry.

When we left the school parking lot with the other two girls and walked to my car, I noticed the small bag of change you were carrying.

I figured that word must have gotten out that our first stop is usually the candy store. I always provide each child with a grub-stake. I figured you brought along some extra to keep yourself in chocolate through the weekend.

Hey, take care of No. 1. People do that all the time.

But no.

You were afraid the other girls wouldn't have enough quarters to buy what they wanted.

So you shared from what little extra money is in the household.

You might only be in the fourth grade, Sierria, but in compassion for your fellow human beings, you're in graduate school.

You had no thought that there would be less for you.

Just that there would be more for your companions.

Obviously, you've been taught well. Just because there's no car at home doesn't mean there's no wisdom.

Generosity is a prized commodity, Sierria. Few people have it. Oh, some folks talk a good game. But when it comes to taking money out of their pocket and putting it in someone else's, well, most stop short.

Your heart will carry you a long way in this world, little girls of the bag.

Even up the hills.

Years ago, when he was sheriff of Muhlenberg County, Ky., I met Harold McElvain, nicknamed "Roadblock" because he weighed close to 500 pounds.

The man left me in stitches.

He's a "good ol' boy" to the power of 10.

Roadblock told me about some of the bad guys he's chased, arrested and run about of town.

Once his girth actually helped solve a case. The sagging floor in a log cabin gave way when he crossed the room, and the lawman spotted the contraband in the underpinning.

I caught up with Roadblock the other day at his office south of Greenville.

"Got out of politics in 1990," he says, drawling and tugging on the suspenders of his bib overalls. "Six years as a deputy. Two terms as a sheriff. That's enough."

The 58-year-old man says he's down to 430 pounds.

"Been trying to watch what I eat."

His business interests include a collection agency, ownership of a race car and antiques. He's also a repo man.

"Probably had 10,000 jobs from here to Ohio. I can get in a truck, pick the lock and be gone in 14 seconds. Had more guns pulled on me than you can fit in this room."

Roadblock takes a telephone call from a repo employee who wonders what to do with a car that was driven into someone's house.

"Pull her out real gentle-like and be quick," the expert advises. "The man doesn't want to lean over somebody's motor vehicle while he's trying to watch television."

Until recently, Muhlenberg was a completely dry county. Bootleggers were all over the place.

"The absolute funniest thing that ever happened was one night when me and my deputy confiscated a big bunch of illegal hootch.

"We went outside to load it up and, lo and behold, here was this goat on the roof of the squad car chewing on the vinyl. He'd dig in with his hooves and pull back as hard as he could. Whole chunks were coming out. Never forget as long as I live. It was a Plymouth Fury. Nothing we could do but watch."

Roadblock says it wasn't uncommon for some of the large-scale bootleggers to earn $20,000 a week.

"They'd haul the stuff in big tractor-trailers that they'd park just outside the county line. Some of the customers were people who didn't have a ride to get to a wet county, but you had some 18-year-olds who bought for the excitement of the moment.

"I still see some of the folks I arrested years ago. They stick out a paw and ask how I'm doing. I never held anything against the bootleggers. I treated 'em with respect. I'd just say, 'Bob, one of us is right and one of us is wrong.'

"Of course, you had some that sold drugs. And you had some that sold to underage. I remember seeing this 6-year-old boy on a bicycle who had a six-pack on the handlebars. He was so little I almost could have put him in my pocket. Told me his father said to go buy it. Followed the kid home and arrested the old man on the spot."

Not long ago, Central City voted itself wet. Harold McElvain says that's reduced the number of bootleggers in the rural county to a handful.

"Sometimes I'd use my wife (Kaye) to make buys. This one bootlegger came to the window and sold her some beer. He looked at her real close and said, 'I'm caught, ain't I?'

"I showed my face and told him, 'Yeah, buddy, you sure are.'"

A great man died the other day.

Art Buchwald.

Oh, you probably don't think so. He was just a guy who wrote a lot of humor columns. You either read his stuff or you didn't. No big deal.

You're teachers, construction workers and salespersons. Accountants, nurses and electricians. Art Buchwald was just another block of type in the newspaper. Nothing important. Not like it was your job or anything.

His three-times-a-week dose of funny stuff was important to me. It was what I wanted to do. Dreamed of, even.

In high school, the few kids who read the newspaper concentrated on sports or the comics.

I clipped Buchwald's columns and tried to figure out why they made me laugh.

In one piece, the setup was a motorist pulled over by a policeman on Thanksgiving. Instead of imbibing excessive spirits, the poor sap was guilty of consuming too much holiday food. The back-and-forth took the tone of a cop questioning a drunk driver by the side of the road, but the punch lines were white meat, dark meat, giblets and bean casserole.

I learned what best describes Buchwald's approach. Comic juxtaposition. That's seven syllables all in a row, thank you very much. Pretty good for a "B" student from Appalachia.

Imitating his style, I wrote columns at Virginia Tech for the student newspaper.

Because I was much too shy to actually show my creations to anybody, I hid in the bushes until the last staffer left for the night. Then, with only the janitor to beat, I raced up the stairs, stuffed my three typewritten pages under the transom and fled into the darkness.

A miracle happened, and some of my columns were published. I sent Buchwald a sampling, making sure the cover letter contained my two newest favorite words. Comic juxtaposition. It was all very moronic, but he wrote me a nice letter.

"Don't get too good. I hate competition."

Buoyed by this encouragement from a fellow sojourner in seven syllables, I spent long hours typing columns and mailing them to editors of big-city newspapers. I just knew there would be a bidding war for my services, and I would end up with a cushy columnist's job in a big office with a rubber plant in the corner.

It didn't happen.

One editor said my piece on the university issuing female students brassieres that glow in the night so lost male students can find their way home made him physically ill. Another said my writing convinced him that, at least for some students, four years of college isn't nearly enough.

But I persevered and landed a position at a small newspaper in West Virginia. No rubber plant, but a clear view of the fading neon light that illuminated every other letter of the "Milner-Matz Hotel" sign. Within a year, I had my own column. Time passed and I eventually did it five days a week.

Not long before coming to Evansville in 1987, I found my original letter to Buchwald. I sent that and a fresh batch of columns and signed it, "the comic juxtaposition guy." He wrote back and said I made him laugh. I wish I had saved it.

For my part, I'm still clipping. The tributes penned about him last week are overflowing my desk drawer.

A great man.

It's almost 11 p.m. So far, the prostitution sting in the North Fares Avenue section of Evansville has gone by the book. See hooker. Arrest hooker.

Five women have been successfully baited by a heavyset undercover patrolman who swallowed fast-food hamburgers the entire time.

The other cops laughed at his technique, all the while reminding him to wipe his mouth.

Meanwhile, John No. 2 – trimmer and driving a Cadillac -- couldn't even score a telephone number.

The other cops laughed at his utter lack of moves.

The women weren't exactly forthcoming about what they were doing.

They professed innocence.

Said it was all a mistake.

One told an especially good whopper about being the girlfriend of the burger-eating undercover officer.

The cops really laughed at that.

I did, too. You sorta get caught up in it.

Then we went across town to the booking room.

One of the arrested women waits for the elevator to take her upstairs to jail where she'll spend the night.

She cowers in the corner behind a set of bars. Even though she's fully clothed, she tries to cover herself with arms and hands.

Her gaze goes to the floor.

Looking for the drain.

Where everything that defines her as a person has gone.

She's gone through the being-handcuffed phase of losing her self-respect. Then the sitting in the restraining chair while waiting for her mug shot to be taken. Then to being just one more name on an arrest warrant.

"We usually delouse them, just as a precaution," a lawmen says. "You never know where they've been."

The woman hears.

All dignity gone.

She slumps to the floor, softly crying.

Naturally, the elevator is in park somewhere.

The woman doesn't have control of anything else. Why should she be able to influence the speed of her ride?

One of the cops tells me the overwhelming majority of prostitutes have drug or alcohol problems.

Rehab, AIDS screening and substance-intervention programs cost money.

Unwilling to work to change the lifestyles of those we consider beneath us, society does what it considers the next best thing.

Which is to form sting units two or three times a year and arrest as many of them as possible.

While trying not to laugh.

The woman waiting to be deloused needs help.

Maybe she has children. Their home life can't be good.

She knows other women who get in cars with strangers in exchange for a cash advance.

They need help.

She knows men who stable prostitutes like so many horses. They never roam far because he doubles as the dope man.

These guys need to go to prison.

But we're slow to react.

Like the jail elevator.

The woman's stay behind bars won't be long. There's only limited space and it's reserved for more dangerous types.

She'll be shown the door.

Untreated.

Unhelped.

Lots of yucks.

MERCURY SABLE

Born in 1994, Mercury Sable passed away today after a long bout with transmission disease along with the complete failure of the engine to achieve anything close to internal combustion.

Survivors include Evan Mathews and his father, Garret, who bought the car on the cheap for his son to take to college. Mercury Sable was a willing hunk of metal, but there are only so many trips to Bloomington, Ind., in any vehicle's constitution.

The end came when large plumes of smoke came up from the hood, enveloping the conveyance in one final cloud of pollution for old time's sake. This was accompanied by a grinding noise that sounded like a demonic eighth-grader let loose in metal shop.

The car jerked to a halt. The dashboard and upholstery called for one final charge, but it wasn't to be. Mercury Sable had thrown oil for the last time.

There was no need for an attending physician. Even an automotive moron whose sole knowledge is where to hang the air freshener knows death in the afternoon when he sees it.

In life, Mercury Sable enjoyed moonlit nights, soft summer mornings and driving downhill.

The car never knew a stranger from the lowliest mechanic to the guy who owns the shop.

The family would like to thank everyone who displayed compassion to Mercury Sable in its last days, but especially motorists who pulled alongside at stoplights and had the good grace not to laugh.

We would also like to thank Jacob Mayberry, whom you'll meet in a few more lines of this obituary.

Ever the imp, Mercury Sable provided one last piece of drama before going to its reward where maybe, just maybe, the car will be reunited with its hubcaps,

The junkyard – and its promise of $75 for Mercury Sable's remains – is seven miles from the Mathews abode.

The car managed to function for six before collapsing by the side of the road. Even after numerous kicks to the area most resembling its groin, Mercury Sable would not turn over.

Mathews and his youngest son began pushing the car toward payday.

Forget everything else you've ever heard about distance. This was the longest mile.

Jacob Mayberry saw the two men, put down his sack of groceries and cheerfully joined in.

"What are you doing?" he asked.

"Beating the tow truck industry out of a gig," Garret Mathews replied.

"Cool."

Several drivers honked their horns at the procession that at times achieved 4 miles per hour.

The family would like to thank those who had the good grace not to extend middle fingers along the route.

Mercury Sable reached the junkyard.

The family would like to apologize for leaving it in the middle of the lot, but we were tired of pushing the darn thing.

Mercury Sable was preceded in death by 1992 Corsica, 1987 Honda, 1977 Buick and 1971 Pinto.

Memorial contributions may be made to the family's lug nut fund.

April 8, 2007
Covering The Bases For Kids' Baseball Coaches

Because my two boys failed to heed my strictest instructions and stay 10 years old for the rest of their lives, April is upon us and I don't have a kids' baseball team to coach.

But you do.

Worry beads the size of boulders have formed on your forehead.

You've closed deals from here to Nepal. You've pushed product in Pomona. You've hung drywall in a hurricane.

But you've never been alone in a dugout with a bunch of fourth-graders.

Tryouts are coming up.

How will you know which youngsters to pick? The games last well into June. How can you be sure your team doesn't lose every game by the mercy rule?

Today is your lucky day, neophyte coaches.

For absolutely no charge, I will share from wisdom gained from more than a decade of watching elementary school students write their names in the dugout dirt.

Not only will I tell you which kids to draft who might actually help you win a game or two, I'll tell which ones to avoid.

Here goes:

Pick a child who has a good-looking mom (GLM). Hey, it's a long season.

Listen carefully when the children are waiting for their turns to hit and field. Do not pick a kid who uses the word "lawsuit."

Choose a kid who can recite "Old Ironsides" from memory. He should be able to remember the signs.

Do not select a child who comes to tryouts wearing a "Dear Abby" T-shirt.

Do not select a child who comes to tryouts wearing shower thongs.

Do not select a child who comes to tryouts carrying a box of doughnuts.

The equipment bag can get heavy. Pick a kid whose father is a powerlifter.

Pick a kid who can burp the vowels. He can entertain the troops while you're getting beat 31-2.

Pick a kid who says he wants to be a pirate when he grows up. He could turn out to be your best baserunner.

Pick a kid who tries to flush his feet down the toilet. See previous item on the need to provide alternative entertainment.

Do not select a child who asks if he can borrow a baseball to dissect for science class.

Pick a kid whose mom or dad play in the Philharmonic. When the season goes down the dumper, you can teach your players a new musical instrument.

Do not select a kid whose father has to tie his shoes.

Do not select a kid who puts marbles in his eye sockets before batting.

Pick a kid with freckles. If you're getting beat 28-4, the other kids can have fun connecting the dots.

Pick a kid whose GLM likes to bring other GLMs to the ballpark. See previous item about the long season.

BOONVILLE, Ind. – The old-timers' basketball game won't start for an hour, but the former Millersburg and Tennyson players are already on the floor – practicing set shots and sneaking looks on the other end of the court to gauge the nimbleness of their opponent.

It's Tuesday night at the Pioneer Classic, a tournament featuring ex-hoopsters from Boonville, Chandler, Elberfeld, Millersburg, Newburgh, Tennyson and Selvin high schools. Several of these communities haven't had prep teams for more than 30 years.

Jim Adams helped assemble Tennyson's squad. It was his idea to put the players' names and the years they graduated on the backs of the white uniforms.

"There's Rufus Smith," Adams says, pointing with his clipboard. "He had heart surgery not too long ago, but he didn't want to miss this. You gotta like that kind of spirit."

If the heavy equipment operator sounds like a coach, he is – at least for the week. At 44, he's also the youngest member of the team. Tennyson High School closed in 1962.

"I'm the only ringer," Adams says. "Every other guy went to the old school."

Which explains the smell of ointment and an assortment of knee pads that look like something that fell out of a Second World War gym bag.

Bill Farmer was the last basketball coach at Tennyson High. Adams thought it would be nice if the 75-year-old man sat on the bench.

"In those days, everybody who came out for the team played, even if the game was close," Farmer recalls as he watches the men do a ragtag version of a layup drill. "It was a small community and the people wanted to see all the boys in action. I didn't have a problem with that."

I asked Farmer to tell me a cracker-box gym story.

"The court over at Richland City had swinging light bulbs. Occasionally, the ball would hit one and glass would fly all over the place. The wooden gym at Yankeetown was heated by pot-bellied stoves that were scalding hot. You had to be careful going after a loose ball in the corner."

One player lights a cigarette. Another tries to adjust his jockstrap that he says is "digging a pit" in his backside.

Adams asks Farmer for advice.

"Remember, dunking is against the rules and the goal won't count," he says, laughing.

Irvin Decker, class of 1945, takes a seat on the bench.

"We didn't have a gym," he recalls, "so practice was a problem. Sometimes we'd have a chance to go to Folsomville, but most times we just went outside. You get a bad snow and we might not get any work for a week or more. I can remember plenty of times shooting baskets when it was well below freezing."

Millerburg's players are taller, faster and less bald. Its team jumps to a 30-11 lead.

Time out. Jim Barnett, class of 1945, takes a seat on the bench.

"I think the players had more support back when we played," he says. "There weren't as many things to do, so people turned out. And they were loyal, too. You could lose big and they'd still show up."

Millersburg continues to increase its lead.

Two of Tennyson's players are talking about cattle. Another says he's going to find an attractive woman to give him a massage.

"So far nobody's gotten hurt," Bill Farmer says. "That's the good thing."

Maybe you missed the wire story about the Glynn County, Ga., Mosquito Control Department.

The coastal county hires six part-time employees to drive to low-lying areas, stand outside for 60 seconds and, for $8.37 an hour, count how many mosquitoes try to bite them.

The idea is to get a fix on the density of the blood-suckers in problem areas and set priorities for spraying.

One of these folks is 22-year-old David McDonald. I got hold of him the other afternoon after his blood supply had clocked out for the day.

Gee, David, what a lousy way to make a living.

"It's not so bad. I get to be outside a lot."

But so do the mosquitoes.

"Yes, sir, and they'll sure bite you, all right."

What's your personal record for a minute?

"Around 100."

Do you just let the things have their way with you, or are you permitted to swat them off?

"The department wants to get a good count, so you're supposed to stand there and go 1, 2, 3, 4. Sometimes I pop 'em, though. I ain't gonna lie about it."

Just guessing, David, but I'll bet time stands still while you're holding forth in a swampy, high-thorax district.

"Yes, sir, when they're swarming, you do get a little anxious."

Do you swell up?

"Not all that much. I rub myself down with alcohol every night when I get home. That seems to help."

This is your second year. Have you picked up any tricks of the trade?

"I can't say that there are any tricks. You just wait until the minute is over so you can go somewhere else."

You're certainly not making much money for being a fleshy dessert. Must be a heck of a benefits package. Right, David?

"The county doesn't take insurance out on us. If we get sick, they don't have to take care of us. There aren't exactly a lot of good jobs around here."

What did you do before becoming a landing zone for every proboscis that comes around?

"Put up fence. You can only put up so much fence."

What do your parents think about their son functioning as mosquito bait?

"They're OK with it. My dad helped get me the job."

Tell the truth, David. Do your friends make fun of you?

"Only some of them."

How many mosquito zones are in the county?

"About 40. I hit each place twice a week."

Do you dress for success?

"They give us long pants and a short-sleeve shirt. The idea is to count the mosquitoes that land on your forearms."

Let's talk welts, David.

"Not all that many. They come and they go. It's not like I have a bunch of scars or anything."

More power to you, pal. I wouldn't last a standing 10-count as a mosquito man.

"It's patience more than anything else. Just stay still until it's time to get back in the truck."

April 13, 2004
Hot Shot Cools Off Hot-Shot Pitcher

The other day I ran into the guy who, many years ago, caused a large red-and-blue wound to appear on my lower abdomen.

Put another way, that part of my body turned into peacock plumage.

I didn't mention it.

To do so would break the back of the lie I've lived since the rainbow first formed.

Flashback to 1992.

I thought it would be fun to spend spring break playing baseball with the Evansville Reitz High School team.

My idea was to participate in drills as if I was a member of the squad. Coach Steve Johnston's reaction was to laugh and say, hey, go for it, you 45-year-old fool.

I ran laps, fielded ground balls, applied a cement mixer's worth of Ben-Gay and drove in a couple of runs in a practice game.

Before I get into the Technicolor injury, let me point out two highlights.

After I sent a line drive up the middle, the first baseman said, "Nice hit, sir."

And then there was the double play.

Runner on first. One out. I was playing second base and hoping the inning ended quickly because I had a rock in my spikes.

Hard grounder to short. My first instinct was relief that it wasn't directed at me.

Then I realized the shortstop expected me to cover second base.

I arrived at the bag just as the 7-foot, 340-pound base-runner (the kid gets bigger every year) prepared to slide with the force of an earth-mover.

Facing certain death, I managed a four-inch vertical leap to avoid the onrushing behemoth and relayed the ball to first base.

Not only did I complete the double play, my knees lived to flex another day.

"Nice throw, sir," the shortstop said.

One afternoon, I volunteered to pitch batting practice.

I successfully stared down the 10-year-olds on my kids' baseball teams. I saw no reason why I couldn't face players with leg hair.

"Ooh, you're a man," Johnston said, obviously impressed.

"That is correct," I replied briskly. "I am a man."

The coach asked if I wanted to pitch behind a protective screen. I declined.

"You seem to forget that I'm a man," I said.

Fast-forward to the fourth batter to step in the box.

I fired my best high hard one. The 8-foot, 420-pound slugger sent it back a la tracer round.

Splat. Ball meets abdomen.

Strike that. Ball obliterates abdomen.

It felt like I had been jackhammered.

But did I wince?

No.

Did I give any indication that my insides had been put in a blender?

No.

Because I am a man.

A stupid man.

That night, I watched the bruise grow an inch an hour.

It was three days before I could bend over without pain.

It was three weeks before I could take off my shirt without answering a lot of dumb questions.

I haven't pitched to guys with leg hair since.

Strict orders from my abdomen.

Friedman Senning is retiring tomorrow after more than 58 years of driving trucks for a living. No more getting up at 2:30 a.m. No more putting his grandchildren on hold.

"I figured I might as well end it on my 76th birthday," the Evansville man says. "I've got close to 5 million miles. That's enough."

This is Senning's second attempt to park himself. This time, he insists, it's for good.

"Twelve years ago, I thought I had enough of the job. Stayed away four months. But not being behind the wheel was making me goofy, so I came back."

He's looking at property in Florida. And then there are his eight grandkids.

"It's getting harder and harder for me to roll the tarp back over my load. That's one thing. I've never turned a truck over. Never put a dent on somebody else's vehicle. Never been laid off. Never got more than about five speeding tickets. It's been a good run."

Senning started out hauling grain in 1948 around his native Washington, Ind.

"Those were long days. No logbook. You could go 16, 18 hours at a time. We'd shell corn during the day and take it to market that night. Your word was your bond back then. You could buy 100,000 bushels and not have to sign a thing."

He remembers breaking down taking a load of white corn to Birmingham, Ala.

"It was 101 degrees and my transmission went out. I found a shade tree behind a filling station and overhauled that thing all by myself. No jack or anything. Twenty-four hours later, I was back on the road."

Senning's first grain truck – a used Chevrolet—set him back $1,800. The 1998 Peterbilt that he'll fire up today cost $120,000. Add another $32,000 for the trailer.

"If you ask me, the best time to make money in the trucking business was the 1970s. You've got a lot more government rules today, plus the high price of fuel and tires."

The Peterbilt belongs to Senning's stepson, Michael Market, who owns a trucking company in Evansville. Most of Senning's trips are early-morning hauls to Springfield, Tenn., with 50,000 pounds of feed ingredients in the back.

"I'm usually home by 2 p.m. I don't run nearly as hard as some of the men."

Has he ever taken pills to stay awake?

"Maybe six bennies in my whole life. I never got in the amphetamines, but there is definitely a lot of dope in trucking. At some of the scale houses, they have drug-sniffing dogs."

Any regrets?

"Over the years, I've probably put out a dozen fires along the side of the road. Maybe a family car. Maybe another truck. Just get out the fire extinguisher and start spraying.

"I don't think I ever saved a life or anything, but I sure took care of the blaze. And nobody ever said thank you. They just took off.

"One time it happened outside Jackson (Tenn.). A few minutes later, the DOT pulled me over to check my safety equipment. I didn't have a fire extinguisher. Just got through using it up helping somebody. Didn't matter. Fined me $68 anyway. That's something I'll never forget."

SPURGEON, Ind. – Most folks shake hands when they're first introduced. Victor Tyring recites.

Poetry. The Bill of Rights. The 94-year-old Pike County man mixes and matches.

"I'm in the Wal-Mart and somebody comes up and I just take off. They're astonished."

The retired farmer grins.

"I guess you could call me an unusual person."

Waving his arms like a stage actor, Tyring starts in on the Preamble to the Constitution.

Gets every line.

Then it's "Little Orphan Annie," the famous work by James Whitcomb Riley.

Gets that, too.

"I probably know a thousand poems from memory. Sometimes I'll slip up on who the author is, but I can get the words. It just comes natural. I don't do anything special to study up except read the newspaper."

His 93-year-old wife, Ida Hazel, sits on a recliner and clutches a lap blanket. A stroke has taken away her speech and hearing.

"We met at the old Spurgeon High School. She was the new girl who came over from Oakland City. Prettiest girl in the room. All the guys tried to get dates with her, but I was the one she picked."

They live in the house he built in 1940 on the family's 600-acre farm.

"Dug the basement with my two-horse team. I've always been a hard worker. That's the only way we got through the Depression."

Tyring still mows his own yard, but daughter Jeannette has taken away his car keys.

"She said I don't notice things too good any more. I didn't think so at first, but I guess she's right."

Tyring recites a friendship poem he likes to share with strangers. A deeply religious man, the verses are about loving the Lord.

"My ability started back in high school. One of the teachers got on me for talking too much when I should be listening. She made me memorize a poem and present it to the class. Thought it would take me a week. I had it licked in a matter of hours."

He instructs his grandchildren and youngsters from the neighborhood on the proper way to memorize the 50 states.

"You start with Maine and work around the edges of the country. Then you go 'round in circles until you get all of 'em in the middle. Here, I'll recite 'em for you."

Gets it.

"What's my secret? I don't know other than to say I can be reading a poem and shut my eyes and still be reading it."

Occasionally, Tyring admits, someone walks away when he's reciting, not interested in the performance.

"I apologize, but I do it again to the next person who comes up."

The smile fades when he looks at Ida Hazel.

"I recite a lot to her even though I know she can't hear. Then I pat her on the head and we hug. She lifts her head up at me. That helps her understand how much I love her."

September 22, 2002
Woman Battles Adversity With Positive Attitude

The doctor told Erna Gordon she needs a new liver.

Go to Indianapolis as soon as you can, he said. Get on the transplant list.

Can't, she replied kindly, as is her way. Don't have the money.

The 53-year-old Evansville woman lives alone in a one-room apartment that's filled with dolls, quilts and flea-market items.

Never been married. Stayed with her parents on the family farm until 1988 when her mother died. Never earned more than $6.25 an hour. No longer sees well enough to drive the 1967 Oldsmobile a friend gave her.

Takes 15 pills a day to combat the auto-immune liver disorder. Vomits a lot. Sometimes her feet go numb and she has to crawl up the steep stairs that lead to her room.

Erna recently learned she has diabetes. Her hair is falling out. She has maybe $10 in the bank.

"For a long time, I worked as a home health aide. Bathe the patients, cook for them, run errands. It was good, but I wasn't getting enough hours.

"So two years ago, I got a job as a grill cook at Weinbach's. Everything was fine until June of last year when my lower body suddenly started swelling up. They told me there was something wrong with my liver, but I'd have to wait until they found out exactly what.

"It hurt to be on my feet, but I kept working. There was rent to pay and groceries to buy. I've never been the kind of person who sticks her hand out."

The swelling worsened and Erna Gordon had to go to the emergency room.

"They ended up pumping out I don't know how many liters of fluid. My blood sugar went way up. One of the nurses said I almost stroked out."

Friends at work said Erna could apply for Medicaid.

She did, but was turned down.

"They said I wasn't sick enough."

The system had spoken. She would listen. Maybe they were right. Maybe she wasn't sick enough.

So Erna Gordon redoubled her efforts to deal with the discomfort and went back to work.

Friends at the store saw how much she was suffering and suggested she contact Legal Aid, an agency that represents low-income persons.

The attorney called last week. The Medicaid ruling had been reversed. She was officially declared disabled and thus able for assistance.

"It was like I finally won at something."

Now she's trying to obtain Social Security disability. The attorney from Legal Aid remains in her corner.

Friends come by occasionally to take her places, but Erna Gordon spends most of her time in the small alcove apartment. The pills make her go to the bathroom a lot, and she doesn't want to be a burden.

Must be a rough life, I noted. To be seriously ill. To be lonely.

"You do get anxious sometimes about how much time you've got left and how much you'll be able to do. He helps to believe in a higher power."

A black cat jumps in her lap.

"This is my baby. Close to 20 years old. Runs up and down the stairs like a kitten. I wish I was so perky."

She smiles.

"When it's my time to leave this world, I won't kick. Just get somebody to keep the cat and I can die happy."

A while back, I did a story on a bunch of mostly military folks who marched 18 miles while toting 25-pound rucksacks. Nobody screamed in pain and the hospital didn't get any new business.

Every so often, I embark on a moronic physical challenge to prove that everyone else on the planet is getting old except me.

The thought hit. Let's put a 25-pound free weight in a backpack and turn into a two-footed pack mule. If I can work up to the 18 miles, I'll petition the Pentagon to make me an honorary general.

I'll take your questions.

So how far did you get on your best day before collapsing in a heap.

Thirteen miles. My feet never hurt so much in my life. Not only did they surrender unconditionally, they joined the other side.

A fiftysomething man walking down the road with an iron weight on his back. You must have looked really stupid.

Yes, especially when I took the thing off in the restaurant and the pack made a loud clang on the table. The manager probably thought I was shoplifting toilet fixtures.

How did your spinal cord hold up?

Fine. I discovered that I have vertebrae to die for. Other than feeling like I was striding on a burst appendix, my problems weren't physical.

What do you mean?

I walked more than four hours. You completely run out of things to think about in that time. Past girlfriends, athletic glory days, Dylan lyrics – I had nothing after 90 minutes.

So what sustained you?

Two things, really. The record amount of food I would soon consume at the all-you-can-eat buffet. And Stonewall Jackson.

The buffet makes sense. After burning up that many calories, you're entitled to devour an entire wildebeest with all the trimmings. But Stonewall Jackson?

I am a student of the Civil War. In 1862, the Confederate leader double-timed his men up and down Virginia's Shenandoah Valley for close to 650 miles in a seven-week span. It wasn't unusual for his "foot cavalry," as the troops were called, to march 15 miles and then go straight into battle without so much as a hardtack du jour.

So you pretended to be one of Jackson's soldiers?

Yes. They had a pack. I had a pack. They trudged. I trudged. The only difference was that iron weights probably hadn't been invented and I eat hardtack for no man.

But at the end of the day's hike, Jackson's boys fought the Army of the Potomac. What did you do?

Spread out on the couch, whined about my feet and watched the Lakers' game.

Could you have engaged in a pitched battle with the enemy?

Lord, no. I barely had the strength to get a beer out of the refrigerator.

So you would have been drummed out of Jackson's brigade?

Yes. I'll put in my eight miles before noon, but I'll require a dessert bar.

Did you see any ambulances during your trek, and were you tempted to hail one?

Saw three. Hailed none. It's the code of the pack animal. Avoid flashing red lights.

Keith Sparks stands confidently in the cook's corner of his kitchen. He finds his mixing bowl and blender. He reaches up to the counter to make sure the seasoning salt and black pepper are in place.

"Steaks, burgers, pies – whatever you want, I can fix it."

The 42-year-old Evansville man is blind.

Sparks routinely walks a mile in any direction from his house on Illinois Street, tapping his white cane to feel for breaks in the sidewalk.

He jokes about being a slow shopper at big-box stores, and how impatient customers have bumped his cart and called out, "What's the matter? Are you blind?"

He breaks into a wide smile.

"I tell them, 'As a matter of fact, yes, I am.'"

Diabetes rendered Sparks completely sightless seven years ago.

"I started going downhill a little at a time, beginning in 1996. There was pain from the pressure, and my eyes felt like I had sand in them."

He had been a cook at several area restaurants, including the Petroleum Club, until his condition worsened.

"I've talked to a lot of blind people, and they tell me about the depression they go through after first losing their sight. That's never been a problem with me. I always look to be positive in life."

That life includes Tammy, his wife of 21 years.

"Our only income is Social Security, and we can't afford a car. We used to spend $150 a month on groceries, and the rising cost of things has almost doubled that. She was with me when I could see, and she stayed when I couldn't. That takes a special person."

Sparks first was diagnosed with diabetes 35 years ago. He's had to call paramedics several times when blood sugar levels soared out of control, sending him into insulin shock.

"I give myself four shots a day. I have to be careful with what I do. I try not to get out in the heat."

They belong to God's Way Church in Evansville and sing in the choir. Church members give them rides to the store.

"It sounds strange to say, but if I wasn't blind I wouldn't have the gladness that I have today. It's made me so much more aware of things around me."

Sparks took some training classes earlier this year at the Evansville Association for the Blind. He practiced jobs he would have at an eatery such as washing tables and pouring coffee.

"That made me think I'd like to work for a restaurant some day. I know I would be limited, but I was a good cook when I could see and I'm still a good cook. And if it's not fixing food, I could help out around the dishwasher as long as I don't have to stack plates."

He walks to the kitchen and shows off what he calls his "work station."

"I can feel the containers of my food preparation supplies and know exactly what they are. Cakes and pies are my specialty, particularly peach and cherry. The other day, Tammy got me a recipe for old-timey mincemeat pie and I cooked it right up."

Keith Sparks recently prepared 48 loaves of bread that he gave away at church.

"I prayed over it and realized they needed the food more than me."

He knows that landing part-time employment at a restaurant is a long shot at best.

"There's the matter of not being able to see, and there is a lot of liability involved. But you won't get anywhere unless you look on the bright side."

Piper Dudley-Bates shows a picture of two of her premature triplets who died shortly after birth.

"The one with the brightest-looking face is Nathaniel. He lived 15 minutes, maybe. We were waiting for him to die, but the poor thing kept doing his best to breathe on his own.

"I asked the nurses, 'Are you sure you can't try something? He's trying hard. Can't you?' They told me he was just too small, too premature. There wasn't anything to do but watch until he passed."

Jordan Kenneth Blackard, the oldest triplet, died Aug. 13. His brother, Nathaniel William, and sister, Marissa Denise Anne, succumbed on Aug. 21. Dudley-Bates was just 22 weeks into her pregnancy.

The Evansville woman was in the hospital from Aug. 5 until Aug. 23.

"I was in a great deal of pain and had a high fever. There was an infection in the umbilical cord. The doctor said if the last two babies didn't get out, the infection would kill me."

At 18 ounces and a little more than 12 inches long, Nathaniel was the biggest. For one picture, a nurse put her hand beside his still body on the bed. He was only slightly longer.

"I made clay molds of their cute little feet. They were a part of me for five months. I don't want to ever forget that."

A friend played 'Amazing Grace' on the bagpipes at the funerals.

"The mortician got Jordan ready first. Then they held him until they found out how many of the other two they would have to bury."

There's not much money in the household. Sunset Funeral Home covered most of the expenses.

She lives with Harold Blackard, 33, in a small rental house. He has three other children from another relationship.

"Harold is always giving me flowers," Dudley-Bates says as she looks at the several arrangements in the living room. "He's good like that."

Donna Cardin is her biological mother.

"I put her up for adoption in 1985," Cardin says. "It was the best thing. My home life wasn't very stable at the time."

Betty Dudley took over custody. The adoptive mother died when Dudley-Bates was 14. She then went to live with Marvin and Denise Bates until getting her own apartment at 17.

"Getting adopted twice. Not many people can say that."

She went to Bosse High School where she was a member of the orchestra.

"I played the violin. It was a nice, relaxing thing to do. I wish I could afford one now."

Early reports on the triplets were good. They had strong heartbeats and seemed to be developing normally.

"My doctor said I was doing better than expected. I was carrying three little ones, and I was still able to get around without a wheelchair. That probably comes from being in pretty good shape after doing martial arts for 10 years."

Piper Dudley-Bates started having contractions after 20 weeks and was put on complete bed rest.

"It just started going downhill, and there wasn't anything anybody could do."

She smiles.

"A lot of people can't understand why I'm not sad all the time. I tell them I had three beautiful kids. Jordan made a face at me just after he was born. You cope by keeping the good things like that in mind."

Young Birthday Boy Enjoys Carrying Extra Load

Congratulations on your third birthday, Evan. I hope you enjoyed the cake and ice cream. Don't worry about the rug. The man at the carpet store said there's a better than even chance that the stains will eventually come out.

There's a more pressing matter that needs your full attention. Potty-training.

It's toddler tradition that when a kid's third birthday rolls around, he gets the hang of the going-to-the-bathroom thing. Simply put, son, he stops carrying a load in his pants.

Evan, I appreciate a good laugh as much as the next father. I found your first 3,000 accidents amusing and, at times, even hilarious. There's something about that "You mean I did it again?" look on your face that cracks me up.

But it gets old after a while, old buddy. I'd much prefer that you make me chuckle by trying to catch a ball or attempting to sing along with Big Bird. You'll find there's quite a wide range of physical comedy in this world. You don't have to limit yourself to toilet mishaps.

Let me be candid, Evan. It concerns me that you don't seem to experience any degree of discomfort after you've gone in your pants. The sheer weight alone should give you pause. But no. It's like you enjoy carrying around the extra baggage,

So far, I've been fairly lucky when it comes to administering to your rear end. When I smell an accident, I make up some hooey about having to leave the house to take care of an urgent matter at work. I shove you in your mother's direction and quickly exit stage right.

She believes she will be banished from the Maternal Order of Mothers if her child is in messy diapers longer than two seconds. She takes care of the matter at hand and I am spared.

Evan, I don't know how much longer I can get away with this. Lately, she's been accusing me of lying when I say I have an urgent matter at work. Worse, she is threatening to withdraw from the

Maternal Order of Mothers. Unless you clean up your act pronto, I might have to.

Let me put it another way, son. One of these days you're going to get interested in girls. One will give you a wink, and you'll head down the path from which there is no return. This is perfectly natural and I won't blame you for it.

But first you have to get that wink. Let me be the voice of experience. Girls will not move their eyelids one centimeter if you are not toilet-trained. I don't care how charming you are or how cute your dimples are. "First things first, buddy," is what they will say.

I'll close with an haute couture reminder. From what I've been able to gather, the look for spring is lean and mean. Bulky is out. If you wear a diaper, you are bulky. If you have used the toilet in the wrong location, you are even bulkier.

Be fashionable. Be potty-trained.

If you can't, well, something just came up and I have to go to the office.

May 11, 1998
'It Ain't Funny None To Me'

In the newspaper business, it's called a "brite" – a story intended to amuse readers.

The circumstances range from the bizarre to the ridiculous. The intent is to give folks a chuckling diversion from the harder-edged news items of the day.

On the surface, the Earl Martin case would appear a classic brite.

On the morning of April 28, the 46-year-old Bluford, Ill., man showed up drunk at the Wayne County Courthouse for the start of his felony drunk-driving case.

The judge suspended the trial and sentenced Martin to jail for criminal contempt of court.

The story appeared in The Evansville Courier and was later sent out on The Associated Press wire for a national audience.

Although the piece didn't come right out and say it, the implication was obvious: A fellow is not exactly doing the smart thing by showing up sloshed for a felony trial in which he stands accused of being sloshed.

I wrote a letter to Martin in the Wayne County lockup, offering to give his side of the story. He called last week.

The fellow admits he has been arrested several times for being drunk.

He admits he "had a few" on the day of his court appearance, but denies that he was "falling-down drunk."

He also denies ever being locked up for anything other than having too much to drink.

"You can run my record on that if you want to."

Let's not kid each other, I said. You have a serious alcohol problem, don't you?

"Yeah, for pretty much all my life. Was in detox over in Mount Vernon (Ill.) for 21 days, but that didn't help.

"Had a knot taken off my chest a few years ago. Doctor said it was caused by alcohol. Said I need to slow down or it will kill me. Got bleeding ulcers, too. That's why I can't do the whiskey any more. Just beer. I sure ain't had no sweet life, you can say that. Cars, possessions, what have you – don't have nothing."

Because you drank too much?

"Yeah."

I asked what he does for a living.

"Run a body shop. I find jobs on my own, too, like painting cars and tractors. They say I'm one of those working alcoholics. Hey, I'm a good body man."

Let's say you get out of jail tomorrow, Earl. What would you do?

"My dad is 84 years old. I'd go to his place and see if he needs anything."

You wouldn't drink?

"Three or four years ago, well, yeah. But now I don't do it every day. And I sure wouldn't do any drinking around Dad."

But you admit you popped a few beers on the morning of April 28 when you went to trial.

"I was nervous…upset. I mean, this was a felony charge."

What do you do when you go out drinking?

"I ain't gonna lie. I'll be there until closing time. But I shoot pool and play bingo, too. It's not always staying at the bar."

I told him about the news item that appeared in our newspaper and, later, on the AP. I told him many people read the story, and no doubt laughed at the person who picked the absolute worst time to go on a toot.

"It ain't funny none to me."

The guy is due to be released on June 28 on the contempt rap, but still faces trial on the felony drunk-driving charge.

"Some things ain't what they say. Like when they put in one report that I was driving under the influence when I was sitting in the back of a pickup in the driveway. Man, I'm fighting that one."

But it is true that you have a problem with booze and it isn't getting any better.

"Yeah."

NEBO, Ky. -- Old friends.

Pete Ayers and Doug Helm met during the Second World War. Helm owned a few cattle trucks and hired Ayers as one of his drivers.

Helm later got in the coal-hauling business. Ayers combined farming and coal mining for his life's work.

Helm sold his last truck two years ago and pronounced himself retired. Ayers walked out of the mines for the final time in 1983.

Helm owned mules most of his adult life. He prided himself on having the finest stock and enjoyed the good feeling that comes with keeping a tradition alive.

He kept pestering his buddy to become a convert. You don't know what you're missing by not having mules, he said. You'll meet new people. You'll see new places.

Very well, Ayers replied. I'll try a couple of animals and see how I like it.

That was 10 years ago. Since then, he's stabled more than 40 mules and traveled as far as Texas to go on wagon rides. The Hopkins County men shared the same age – 70 – but little else.

Doug Helm loved to laugh. Trucking, farming, life in rural America – he had hundreds of stories. Pete Ayers is quieter. Ask a question and he'll give the briefest of answers. If you want to hear more, you'll have to ask another question.

Helm wasn't a collector of mules. If a pair worked together, he'd keep the animals until they died. Ayers is a trader. Buy today, sell tomorrow. The four mules in his barn know better than to take out a long-term lease.

The two men became even closer friends when Ayers left the mines. A spontaneous man by nature, Helm was always ready to go on a wagon ride.

Right now? Ayers would ask.

What's to stop us? Helm would say.

Usually nothing. They'd pack their wives and a few provisions and take off down the road.

Helm was the first to join the Greenbrier Wagon Club, a group of mule and wagon lovers from Tennessee and Kentucky. Members host rides and swap secrets on the care and keeping of their animals. Sometimes they stay out as long as a week, sleeping in motor homes that follow the convoy.

Doug lived for those get-togethers, Ayers liked to say. It was almost as if he was having a family reunion.

Two years ago, a Hopkinsville, Ky., man of their acquaintance died. He asked that his casket be carried to the cemetery on the back of a mule wagon.

Helm and Ayers did his bidding. The procession stopped in the middle of town and the man's body was transferred from limousine to buckboard for the ride to the graveyard.

Tears welled in Doug Helm's eyes. Promise me, he said to his old friend, that this is what will happen when I pass away. Your wagon, your mules. One last ride together.

Ayers nodded.

Helm suffered from diabetes and had poor circulation. He underwent surgery to remove fluid from his lungs. His vision began to fade. His big toe had to be amputated.

This spring, an early-morning fire burned his barn. Two of his mules were killed.

He really started going downhill after that, Ayers said. It was a lot harder to make him laugh.

The old friends went on a 22-mile ride in Ridgetop, Tenn., on June 6. Helm apologized for not being strong enough to harness the mules. Ayers lifted him into the seat. Don't worry about it, he said.

Doug Helm died on June 14.

Grace Helm, Doug's wife of 50 years, called Ayers. Do you remember what he told you that day in Hopkinsville?

The quiet man said he sure did.

The funeral procession left Madisonville for Nebo, eight miles away. The hearse stopped at Doug Helm's house where the casket was transferred to the back of Pete Ayers' mule wagon for the half-mile procession to the cemetery.

Helm was buried in his overalls. Several mourners were dressed in similar fashion.

"That's what he wanted," Pete Ayers said.

Old friends.

ZION, Ky. – The atomic bomb fell on Nagasaki, Japan, a little before lunch on Aug. 9, 1945. More than 74,000 persons were killed. About that many were wounded in the second bombing of a Japanese city in three days. The Second World War was soon over.

A 14-year-old schoolgirl was among the living, despite being less than a mile from the epicenter. She followed the air raid drills she learned in school. Hit the ground immediately. Cover your eyes and ears. Don't look up.

Hundreds of people perished around her. Multi-story buildings were reduced to rubble. Train tracks were ripped from their moorings.

The dazed schoolgirl walked the four miles to her home. She was greeted with hugs by a family who thought she was dead. It wasn't until they touched her that the schoolgirl realized she had been severely burned on the back and arms.

The young lady studied English and became a translator. In 1951, during the Korean War, she met Don Allen, an Air Force man assigned to her sector. They married two years later and he brought her back to his native Henderson County, Ky.

Today, Don and Aiko Allen still live on the 1,000-acre spread. Her five brothers and sisters still live in Nagasaki. She telephones them on a regular basis and visits every January.

Mrs. Allen is a slight woman who smiles a lot and likes to bake cakes for visitors. I asked the 61-year-old woman to talk about the bomb.

"In school, we were brainwashed to believe Japan was winning the war. A soldier would come in unannounced and stand in the back of the classroom. If he heard someone say our country was going to lose, that person would go to jail.

"All the young men had been taken away, so they trained us with spears. When the Americans came, we were supposed to charge at them with our sticks. You had to fight until the last person died. It didn't matter if the Americans had machine guns.

"On the morning of August 9th, I was sick and my mother took me to the doctor. I left his office and went to the train station to get back to my job. It was very crowded and I couldn't catch a train. I started walking to the next station. I heard a plane and saw a shiny object on the end of a parachute (later determined to be a device to measure the effectiveness of the A-bomb). I was thinking about how unusual a thing that was when I saw a big flash and felt a blast wave that was much worse than any tornado.

"At first, I was numb. The sky was suddenly full of smoke and dust. The air felt like scalding oil. Dead people were all around me, most of them completely naked and with no hair. The bodies were so badly burned you couldn't tell the men from the women. The only part of a building I could recognize was a chimney."

She cries.

"I ran to a bomb shelter. I was very scared and very disoriented. Then I saw a man whose skin hung down like the stripes in a shirt. Everybody was so hot and everybody was so confused.

"Nothing was left of the train station except the steel poles. There were no survivors on the train I was supposed to catch. It took me six hours to walk home. There were no landmarks to follow. You couldn't tell what was a street and what used to be a building. Fires were all over the place. There were people stacking bodies on cots like they were logs. Later, the bodies were burned. The odor was horrible.

"I went to a hospital, but there was no medicine. A woman was singing a lullaby to her baby. She was hurt too bad to notice that her baby was dead and had a big piece of glass sticking out of her back."

Aiko Allen's face was blistered for several years and the scars are still visible on her back and arms. "Sometimes I have nightmares. I dream that I hear this plane and then I start to run for the bomb shelter. My husband has to wake me to tell me I am in America now and that won't ever happen again."

August 14, 1990
Only TD Cinches Game, But Glory?

This is the story of a touchdown scored on an early autumn night in 1964 by the 104-pound quarterback of the Abingdon High School junior varsity football team. It was the only time the lad ever made it into the end zone.

I was that signal-caller. My father was the varsity's head coach.

Dad was good at his job, winning several district championships.

I wasn't so hot at mine. I was the slowest and smallest kid on the team. I was the only guy who couldn't rip adhesive tape with his bare hands. Running a lap around the track in full uniform was a journey across the sands of time. The team manager laughed when I tried to put my jersey in the dirty clothes pile after a game. He said I'd have to get grass stain on it first.

Our team consisted of freshmen and sophomores – flawed individuals all -- who weren't good enough to play varsity.

My wide receiver wouldn't snap his chinstrap because his mother told him it caused blackheads.

The tackle and guard on the left side of the ball almost lined up in the backfield so they could be as far from enemy linemen as possible.

Varsity players were hailed wide-mouthed because only varsity players had hair on their legs. Varsity players never practiced in green socks. Varsity players wore top-of-the-line shoulder pads. Ours flapped. They were like cowbells, the coaches putting them on us so we wouldn't get lost.

There was no national anthem before jayvee games. Weary cheerleaders who had just worked the eighth-grade game cheered. Weary referees who had just worked the eighth-grade game refereed.

The concession stand was closed. Halftime entertainment was provided by elementary school kids playing at midfield with a ball they fashioned from a milk carton.

Dad attended this game as he did all JV affairs. He carried a clipboard that spelled out the week's depth chart. I used to sneak into his room at night and peek to see where I was listed. I was always third – by my last name, like everybody else – behind the two varsity signal-callers. Sometimes there was a question mark off to the side.

We were ahead 7-6 going into the last quarter. As always, I called a conservative game, running plays up the middle and around end by my halfback and fullback. Never my own number as I was much too fragile to be tackled.

The Falcons marched down the field for the clinching touchdown. Our linemen were snarling and my backs were never better. We bulldozed the ball to the enemy's 1 yard line.

First and goal. Our coach's neck veins were popping out. My father was looking at his clipboard.

It was now or never. The perfect time for me to score my first touchdown.

I figured I would be reasonably safe if I ran the quarterback sneak over center and right guard. The defense on that part of the line looked particularly demoralized and, besides, I had written several history papers for those two teammates and they owed me a favor.

My strategy was decidedly dirty pool. My running backs' jerseys were covered with blood and mud. Each was itching to make up for all the discomfort by diving over for the score. My uniform was only slightly brown on the backside where I slipped once after handing off.

Their faces dropped when I called the sneak and they grumbled aloud as they took their positions. I was afraid they would purposely jump offside and sabotage my plans, knowing I would never be so bold from the 6 yard line.

But they did nothing to foul up my moment in the moon. I took the ball from center, closed my eyes and stumbled into the promised land. I rolled around more than necessary to make sure I got plenty of grass stain on my jersey.

The few fans roared. The weary cheerleaders called out my name. My father wrote something on his clipboard.

I put my uniform in the dirty clothes pile. The manager let it go. Either it really warranted a dose of detergent or he was one jersey short of a load. He never did say which.

U.S. Experience Can't Compete With Love Of Home

Jasmin Karapancev, our foreign exchange student, left the other day to return to his native Macedonia.

We had the delightful young man on loan for four wonderful months. Now he can put the English on hold, and get back to saying the more natural "Dobre den" when he wants to say, "Good day."

While with us, he fired a shotgun for the first time, visited the Opryland Hotel in Nashville, misplaced his sunglasses 500 times, climbed the rocks at the Garden of the Gods, visited the Chattanooga Aquarium, misplaced his algebra book 400 times, went to a rodeo, ate fried shrimp for the first time, learned how to bench-press, learned how to play Texas Hold-'Em, misplaced his flip-flops 300 times and played Macedonian rap music for middle school students.

Jasmin might be the most social person I've ever met. There could be a party in Cell Block 3 and he'd want to go.

On weekend nights when nothing was going on, it broke his heart – and mine – to stay home.

Macedonia, about the size of Vermont, was formed after the break-up of the Yugoslavian Republic in 1991.

There is ethnic strife in his country caused by the large Albanian population, and fed by the mistrust between the Christian Orthodox and Muslim religions.

Jasmin's adjustment to America was much more difficult than foreign exchange students from more developed nations.

Extortion, the young man told me, is common in his country. Business owners pay protection money to what he calls "Mafia-types."

Powerful men in Macedonia can say the word, Jasmin says, and those who cross them will be beaten up or even killed.

Crime is rampant. Jasmin was amazed to see free-standing vending machines in Evansville, noting that in Macedonia thugs would disable the units and steal the money.

Bribes are a part of everyday life, from avoiding traffic tickets to paying a doctor to declare your son unfit for military service.

The rules on drinking and smoking and young people staying out late are much more relaxed in Macedonia.

Jasmin told me it's not unusual for a teacher to dispatch his students to buy bottles of liquor.

The average Macedonian is too poor to travel abroad. Jasmin told me the country's hotels and car-rental agencies are almost totally dependent on visitors from the United States.

They wear our clothes, listen to our music and go to our movies.

But Jasmin says Americans are not held in particularly high regard.

We're considered arrogant, he explained. We think we're better than everyone else. We make little effort to learn the culture and language of other nations.

Still, he loved going to affluent neighborhoods around Evansville and posing for pictures outside the houses.

My friends won't believe this standard of living, he told me.

Jasmin was amazed at how well Americans behave in restaurants.

It's routine in his country, he said, for loud arguments to break out among dining patrons.

He said too many of his countrymen throw trash on the street and otherwise behave like rednecks.

He said he was embarrassed when British soccer star David Beckham came to Macedonia and was spat on by unruly fans.

Given these negatives, I asked if he would rather live in the United States.

Jasmin shook his head.

"I am a patriot," he said proudly.

One of my favorite movies is, "The Good, the Bad and the Ugly."

Awesome music. Body count in the hundreds. Anti-war theme. Crude and socially unacceptable behavior.

Something for everybody.

I talked by telephone with Eli Wallach, the New York-trained stage actor who played Tuco, "the Ugly."

"The filming was hard work – 16 tough weeks – but I'll remember it as one of my favorite movies. The people seem to like it, too. I'll be walking down the street and somebody will holler for me to say, 'Don't die, Blondie.' (One of Tuco's lines). I usually end up doing it."

The movie was called a "spaghetti Western" because of its predominantly Italian cast whose dialogue had to be dubbed. Clint Eastwood, Lee Van Cleef and Wallach were the only crew members who spoke English.

"The guy opposite me in a scene would count backward from 1 to 10 in Italian, and then I would say what I was supposed to say," Wallach recalled. "I got used to it after a few days. Language wasn't as much a problem as you might think."

I thought the movie was filmed entirely in Italy. Wrong. Sequences involving western towns were shot in Rome, but the rest of the location work was in Spain.

"We stayed in little hotels by the sea and swam in the Mediterranean," said Wallach, who is still active both in movies and on stage.

I asked him to talk about Eastwood.

"A bright man. Very well-read. Good to work with."

What about Sergio Leone, the imaginative director of "The Good, the Bad and the Ugly?"

"Ahead of his time. He wanted to show the Civil War as it really was, so he cast as many amputees as he could. He insisted on using authentic cannon, and the uniforms were exact copies of designs he saw in a military museum.

"Leone and I communicated mostly in French and Italian. He

would keep the camera rolling and didn't mind if actors improvised. There weren't any zoom lenses back then. I can recall trying to hold my position while the cameraman changed equipment."

Wallach said he never heard a note of the brilliant music until weeks after filming was completed.

"I don't receive residuals when 'The Good' is shown on television. There was talk of a sequel, but Leone would not yield the film rights."

In the movie, Tuco is a low-life who has committed every crime known to a judge. He shoots a guy while taking a bath. He steals from a feeble gunsmith. He beats a guy to death with a rock.

"The most difficult scene to film was when I had to lie down beside the railroad tracks and let a train cut the wrist chain that connected me to the dead prison guard.

"They used a dummy on the tracks, but that's really me only a few inches from the train. I almost got decapitated on the first run-through. Leone asked me to do it again and I did, but I was crouched over so far that he couldn't see my face. I said I had had enough of the train. They ended up printing that first take."

What about the desert scene in which a well-watered Tuco is marching a parched Blondie to his death?

"The horse insisted on throwing me, not once but twice. I said they should get rid of the animal, that it was dangerous. The wrangler came over and popped the horse in the nose. After that, there were no more problems."

I asked Wallach how many times he has seen the movie.

"Three. I watch it with my grandchildren. They get a big kick out of it."

I read the other day that Tiny Tim recently released a country song titled "Leave Me Satisfied." The head of the record company said he's confident Tiny will get a good response "because he's truly amazing. He can sing anything."

You remember Tiny Tim. He's the funny-looking guy with the falsetto voice who two decades ago sold a ton of copies of "Tiptoe Through The Tulips." If that's not enough to jolt your memory cells, he married his beloved Miss Vicky on The Tonight Show, a program that remains one of Johnny Carson's highest-rated shows.

Alas, his career faded. Singers with stringy hair, big noses and large foreheads were OK in the 1960s days of peace marches, but newer audiences don't want their crooners to look like an unkempt lawn.

I remember Tiny was scheduled to perform in Roanoke, Va., not long after he pledged his troth to Miss Vicky, but the show was canceled when fewer than 200 tickets were sold.

Down, down, down went his career. Two years ago, he hooked on with the Great American Circus that sets up its tent mostly in small communities. He gave two 15-minute shows a day, alternately singing and strumming his ukulele. He had to make his own travel arrangements.

The circus came to Honaker, Va., a little town about an hour from Bluefield. I made arrangements to interview Tiny in his motel room. Guys in the newsroom thought I was wasting my time. They said his career was a big joke, and how could he expect the public to take him seriously when he doesn't take himself seriously?

I wasn't so sure about that. Maybe it's this feeling I have for underdogs, but there's always been something about Tiny Tim (born Herbert Khaury) I admire. I guess it's his childlike innocence and his unrelenting drive to make it in show business despite all odds.

A smiling fellow in dyed red hair, running shoes, baggy yellow pants and red suspenders opened the door at the motel. It was like going back to 1970. Tiny Tim hadn't changed a bit. He looked the same as when a tuxedoed Carson led a solemn processional in front of NBC's cameras.

He wouldn't tell me how old he is, but said 55 is "close." Neither would he tell me how much the circus was paying him, but admitted to not earning enough to stay two months ahead on the rent. He said Miss Vicky left him not long after the wedding, and that the divorce became official five years later despite his protestations.

We talked about women and relationships. Tiny does not require a rigid church ceremony to consider himself married. It's sufficient in his mind if he puts his hand on the Bible and makes a vow.

He told me he has had four wives since Miss Vicky with Miss Jan the most recent. He turned sad. It seems Miss Jan was traveling with him until a week before the circus reached southwest Virginia. Apparently her devotion started to waver when the water pump and the air conditioning went out on his trailer. She left and he has no idea where she went.

He shrugged big shoulders and showed me the Bible he keeps beside the bottle of Loving Care in his suitcase. He pulled out the ukulele that has electrician's tape on the bottom and checked it for wear and tear. He talked about how Satan is winning the battle on Earth, and how he telephones his mother in New York every day.

I asked about the circus, and he said he thinks of it as an important career move. He said he still believes he has talent, and that it is still possible to have another hit record.

I asked if Honaker was the end of the line, the absolute farthest one can be from the bright lights of Manhattan.

He smiled and said all places look the same – Honaker and Las Vegas – if you stay inside the hotel room all the time.

I asked Tiny Tim if he believes there is another Miss Jan out there somewhere. He turned sad again.

"If I die right now, I will die unfulfilled because I have been a failure at love. I don't know how to keep a woman."

He played some songs on the battered ukulele until it was time to leave for the show. I wished him well and meant it.

Tiny Tim died in 1996.

MONTGOMERY, Ind. – It's 3 o'clock, the end of the school day at the Amish community a few miles outside this Daviess County town. Some of the children board buggies. Those who live within eyeshot of home – including 14-year-old Jeremy Raber – trudge down the road.

His parents, Leon and Mary, operate a dairy farm. They own 40 acres and work another 60. Leon helps his brother, Owen, repair outbuildings on the latter's property damaged by a recent tornado.

Jeremy's barn chores begin before down, the only light coming from a miner's lamp.

The oldest of seven children looks in the storage cellar to check on the potatoes. If a section of fence is down, he'll join the repair crew.

Classes at the two-room school start at 8:30 a.m. Jeremy is in the eighth grade, the end of formal Amish education. Next year, he'll stay home and help his father.

Report cards came out this day. Children are given numeric grades in a dozen or so subjects to include German and memory work.

Leon Raber looks at the yellow sheet and nods approval.

Evening chores end around 7 when supper is served. Bedtime is usually about two hours later.

After a quick snack, Jeremy puts on a pair of wading boots and walks to the barn.

The young man prepares buckets of grain for the heifers, and then climbs to the loft to throw down bales of hay for the horses.

The Belgians walk slowly toward the barn.

"They take their hay from the same place every day," Jeremy says. "It's like they have a rule."

Dog Spot has been around long enough to know the wisdom of keeping one's distance while the horses are feeding. Skippy, a recent addition, gets too close and narrowly escapes a head butt.

The horses take their leave and the heifers are brought in.

Leon Raber shovels mud outside the barn. He teases Jeremy, noting that while the older boy was sick, his 5-year-old brother, Seth, took his place in the barn and "threw down silage just as good."

I ask what they do for fun.

Leon mentions going to Dinky's (a local auction barn) to trade rabbits. He says the young people get together for a Sunday night social and play volleyball.

Jeremy, his father notes proudly, is a "big reader."

The boy smiles shyly, not wanting to be the center of attention.

"Mostly mysteries," Jeremy says, "and stories about dogs."

I ask the youngster if he's ever been on the Internet.

He shakes his head.

I pose the same question to Leon Raber and get the same answer.

"Some farmers use it to buy commodities. My farm's not big enough to make it worthwhile."

We talk about his children staying in the faith when they become of age.

"I hope they all do, but I know it's hard."

There's an awkward silence. I'm an outsider. Best not talk too much.

Leon Raber looks down at the thick layer of mud.

"It's too warm outside," he says, changing the subject. "Give me ice any day."

And returns to his shoveling.

NORTONVILLE, Ky. – Herman Moore finishes his supper of white beans, scooping stragglers with a piece of white bread.

The 80-year-old retired coal miner takes out his false teeth to eat his dessert of strawberry pie. Then he counts the five pills he takes to combat diabetes, arthritis and poor circulation.

"I started hand-loading coal in 1939 at the No. 6 Rogers Mine at White Plains (Ky). Some places were high enough for you to stand up a three-foot scoop shovel and some weren't. Some men would lean over with their backs against the top, but it was better for me to get on my knees. You didn't straighten up from 7 when you went down in the mine until you got out at 3:30."

The Hopkins County man didn't go back to school after the third grade. He was glad then but is sorry now. His daughter helps him pay bills. He can't read well enough to get much out of his Bible.

"They paid us 40 cents for each ton of coal we loaded. We furnished our own powder and our own fuses and set our own props. If the top came down on your head, you knew it was your own doing. We'd blast the coal every night so we'd have something to work with the next morning. Ponies pulled the coal cars in and out of the mine. They pulled good. You never had to beat 'em."

Moore hand-loaded at the non-union Rogers mine for two years before taking a job at a mine in Dawson Springs, Ky., that had machines to run the coal. He worked on the railroad and on the farm before returning to the mines as a tipple man. He retired in 1972.

"On a good day, you could hand-load 10 tons. It depended on how fast the ponies could get the full car out and bring an empty car in. We had it pretty good at No. 6. They wouldn't dock you for loading gob or rock like they did at other mines. The men outside knew it was my coal because each man had his own chip that you put on the side of your car. My number was 115."

The radio in the kitchen is set on the gospel station. The preacher talks about eternity and the grace of God and the wisdom that's in the book of John. Moore listens to the prayers for the shut-ins while he eats.

"You worked with a buddy when you hand-loaded coal. I had three at No. 6 and not a one was lazy. The best was a man who only had one leg. He fell off a train when he was a boy and got hurt bad. He only had a few fingers on his right hand and his left leg was a seven-inch stump. That never bothered him, though. He had a long pair of crutches that he used to get inside the mine and a short pair that he used when he got to his work. He'd prop himself up on his good leg and shovel like a fool.

"I was young back then and the bending over didn't bother me much. Your back didn't get a break the entire time you were inside, not even at lunch. You sat on a lump of coal and ate your food. The carbide lamp gave you about 15 feet of light. Your world didn't amount too much.

"Some mines would brag about hand-loading records to make the men dig more coal. You'd even hear of prizes the operators would give. They didn't happen at No. 6. They didn't have enough mine ponies to keep you working all the time. You'd scoop all you could and then you'd have to wait. You weren't making any money. But at least you got the chance to take a rest.

"You paced yourself is what you did. You didn't race to see how fast you could get that car filled. You worked enough to keep the shovel moving. There were a lot of coal cars. You only had the one back.

"People ask me sometimes if hand-loading was a good way to make a living. There weren't many choices back then, I tell 'em. They were Hoover times and you either worked or starved. There wasn't any welfare or food stamps. It didn't matter whether you looked forward to going to the mines or not. You went anyway.

"If I had my life to live over, I wouldn't work as hard. I'd get more education and I'd spend more time singing. That used to be a real pleasure for me, but I smoked too much and there's nothing left of my voice. If I was a young man, I'd go to singing school. I'd have something that nobody could take away."

December 20, 2000
She Bumps And Grinds To Support Kids

I'm in the Busy Body Lounge in Evansville talking with Sara, an exotic dancer who wants to be a herpetologist.

Or trying to talk with her.

Alice Cooper's "Elected" is blasting my eyeballs out, an old guy at the next table is getting one heck of a lap dance, and a man I don't know is whispering in my ear that I should go with him if I want "some real chick action."

Sara (who wouldn't give her last name) says she is divorced and living in Henderson, Ky. At 29, she is one of the oldest of the two dozen or so women who take their clothes off here. She says she was working as a receptionist, but the company downsized and she not only lost her job, but the car and the place where she was living.

"I had to let on about this to somebody in the family, so I told Mom. After she got over the shock, she said, 'Lord, child, don't tell Dad.'"

Sara keeps close watch on who walks in while she is performing.

"If I see somebody who doesn't have any business knowing what I do, I put on a Jason hockey mask."

I ask if her three boys, the oldest of whom is 11, know what she does for a living.

"To them, I'm a waitress. When they get a little older and better able to understand, I'll come clean."

Her per-hour pay is minimal, only $2.50. But she sometimes makes $850 per week in tips.

"I'm giving myself another eight months of this and then I'll go back to college. Study reptiles. Now that would be cool."

Sara is wearing three, maybe four ounces of clothing. She throws back her long black hair and asks if I think she looks good.

Well, uh, yes.

"Honey, let me tell you I wasn't in much condition when I started. But you dance for six hours a day, six days a week and you get in shape."

I allow that she sure is in shape all right.

"Go ahead. Feel my thighs."

If you insist.

"Tight as a drum. Don't want the other girls to think I can't keep up."

Sara says she has 10 different outfits and that some cost more than $100. The high heels retail for $80.

"I go to specialty shops mostly. You can't buy this stuff off the rack."

Let's take a typical Saturday night. How many times are you propositioned?

"At least 10. Some guys think because I dance that makes me a prostitute. I try not to be rude. I just say I have to go home to my kids.

"It's not a dignity thing with me. I am completely in charge of what happens on that stage. How many people can say they are completely in charge at their work?

"If people choose not to look at me as an intellectual person, I'm not the least bit bothered. I'll just go home and take out the night's money. It's like a little game. For every person who doesn't approve, I take out another 20-dollar bill."

I ask if she feels sexy while dancing.

"Not with the moves, but with the music. Like tonight it was the Doors. I close my eyes and really get into the words."

Could this line of work come back to haunt you in 10 years?

"Only if I decide to go into politics."

I ask what she's going to do when she gets home.

"Catch up on my sewing. I'm way behind."

July 1992.

My oldest son's baseball team was playing another group of 11- and 12-year-old boys across town.

I noticed the youngster early in the game. He was smaller than the other children on their team and seemed to lack confidence. He played a deep, deep right field so he could be as far from batted balls as possible.

It was the last inning of a tournament game and our bunch had the lead. Their first two kids failed to hit. The last batter in the game – and his team's season – would be the little right fielder.

The boy missed the first two pitches badly and walked away from the plate. Not to fetch another bat. He wanted to get out of there. Away from the pitcher. Away from everyone who was watching him.

The adults in the dugout convinced him to give it another try. Against his better judgment, the child returned to the batter's box. There were tears in his eyes.

The boy held the bat against his shoulder.

Strike three.

He cried so hard his entire body shook.

"I hate myself, I hate myself," he hollered.

There was little joy in our team's victory. All I could see was that little boy's water-stained face.

I wrote about the sad end to the game, urging the youngster to put it behind him.

Keep trying, I concluded. Your time will come.

Fast-forward to last week.

I received a telephone call from Tim Swickard, a proud father.

"Do you remember the piece you wrote a long time ago about the little right fielder from West Terrace who struck out in the big game and started crying?"

It began to come back to me.

"You never mentioned his name, but we all knew what you

meant. It's my son, Brian. His Army National Guard unit just got back from Afghanistan. Maybe you'd like to talk with him."

I met with the young man at the University of Southern Indiana where he's studying chemistry.

"Our unit was in charge of security outside Kabul. Anything that went outside the wire from convoys to humanitarian aid, we were the go-to guys."

Brian Swickard wears a buddy bracelet in memory of a friend, Norman Snyder, who died in an explosion.

"The scariest time was when these Afghans with big guns suddenly surrounded our Humvee. They thought we were a threat to their warlord. Our interpreter finally straightened it out, but if anybody had stepped wrong, it would have been a nasty situation."

I showed him a copy of the 1992 column.

"That season was the first time I ever played baseball. I was scared I was gonna get hit. When I reached base, it was usually because I scrunched down at the plate and got walks.

"It wasn't too bad during the regular season, but I didn't want to make the last out in the tournament. That was too much pressure."

Brian remembers his coach getting the boys together after the game and thanking them for a good season.

"He had his arm around me and that made me feel better. Mom and Dad took me out for dinner that night. They said what happened was like falling off a horse. I'd have to get back on next year."

And did you?

Brian Swickard beams.

"I had a great season. I played second base and pitched. I don't mind saying it. I was the cornerstone of the team."

September 22, 1992
Phone Operators Have A Lot To Talk About

JASPER, Ind. – The 10th annual telephone operators reunion will be held Friday night at the Knights of Columbus Home.

They'll talk about the fire in 1957 that damaged much of the equipment in the Jasper office. And the dawning of the computer age in 1962 when consoles began to replace the cords and brass plugs. And the sad day in 1983 when the operators were transferred from Dubois County to Seymour, Ind.

Contel and GTE came later. The memories that will be savored Friday night date back to the 1940s and 1950s when the boss was the Indiana Telephone Corp., and operators wore weighty metallic headdresses that, one recalled, made her look like a unicorn.

About 30 women are expected to attend.

Mary Suhs, 63, of Jasper, will be among them. She was an operator for 30 years, retiring in 1987.

"The signal button would light up and I'd pick up the phone and say, 'Number, please.' The person would give it to me, and then I'd reach over and put the plug in the proper jack. If I got static, I'd tell them the line was busy.

"We had 60 or 70 operators on rotating schedules. You might work three days and then turn around and work three nights. It was definitely a manual labor job. You did a lot of reaching to put the plugs in. In an average hour, you'd pull way more than 100. There was an art to it. You had to answer one call while another one was ringing."

Mary says she never missed a day due to bad weather.

"We had a terrible storm about 15 years ago, the worst I've ever seen. Way below zero and four feet of snow. Someone from personnel picked me up at the bottom of the hill. I left the house with my blanket and told my husband don't you dare take your eyes off me. I could have taken a bad step and disappeared forever in those drifts. Nobody complained, though. We knew what we were doing was important. Nobody wanted to make excuses about why we couldn't come in.

"The reunions are special because we worked together on Sundays, at nights and on holidays. We became like family and, like family members do, we want to keep up with each other."

Jane Bartley, 64, went to work for the phone company in 1947, earning 75 cents an hour. The Jasper woman retired in 1983.

"The absolute worst time was the day President Kennedy died. Any operator would tell you that. I came to work at 1 p.m. and the white lights on the board were lit up like a Christmas tree. People were numb. The only thing they knew to do when they heard the news was to call somebody. The volume was so bad that fuses were blowing out all over the place.

"There wasn't any 911 service back in those days, so it was up to the telephone operators to contact the firemen," Mrs. Bartley recalls. "We'd run down the list and if the line was busy, we'd interrupt and say there was an emergency call."

Could you still pull the plugs? I asked.

"Absolutely."

Ruth Schuetter, 60, of Jasper, retired recently after 42 years.

"Long ago, we got a call on a 10-party line from a woman who lived in rural Dubois County. I couldn't make out what she was saying because she sounded confused. It had to be bad, like a stroke or something. Our equipment people found out where she lived and we relayed the information to the sheriff. He went out there and broke her door down to get inside. Turned out she had a cerebral hemorrhage and they took her to the hospital in Evansville. She went into a coma and died the next day.

"Later that week, I got a call from a member of the family thanking me for trying to save the woman's life. That was good to hear. I never looked at being an operator as just another job. I always thought we were something special."

I was riding my bicycle past the nursing home when an ambulance pulled up, its lights flashing.

The attendants rushed inside the building and came back a few seconds later with a tiny woman who didn't fill half the gurney. An oxygen mask was on her face to supplement the tube on her nose. A nurse was taking her pulse.

The elderly woman had no expression in her eyes. The gurney banged into the side of the ambulance as she was being loaded inside. The patient didn't move.

"This is her second time this month," I overheard someone say. "Don't think she's gonna make it."

Its contents properly sealed, the back door slammed shut and the emergency vehicle sped away.

I thought about the finality of it all.

Whatever the woman held dear is gone.

A favorite quilt, perhaps.

Or a stuffed animal.

Or maybe the greeting cards she received last Christmas that the nursing home staff put on display in the front lobby.

Boxed, crated and given to the next of kin.

Whatever the woman was good at, she'll never be good at again.

Work force skills such as keeping a room full of second-graders on task, perhaps.

Or balancing the books at the store.

Or stitching pants legs at the clothing factory.

Maybe the tiny woman's specialty was hearth and home.

Maybe the things she was good at in her younger days didn't merit a paycheck, but were important just the same.

Remembering all the birthdays and anniversaries in the family.

Stacking vestments at the church.

Having the cleanest kitchen floor on her side of town.

Gone.

As she became older, she had to find other things to be good at.

Things within the realm of someone who lives at a nursing home.

Doing crossword puzzles, perhaps.

Or helping new residents adjust to assisted living.

Or keeping a fresh smiley face on the table by her bed.

Gone.

No appeal play for more time on this Earth.

No do-over.

Just the back of the ambulance.

I wondered if the woman made a list of everything she wanted to accomplish before she died.

And if just last week she put a checkmark by the last item.

Or if there are another two pages that she never got around to.

I thought about my own life.

And time that I wasted when I was convinced the mortality tables were for everybody but me.

I thought about gray hair and sore knees and other body parts that sometimes ache for no reason.

I thought about being strapped onto a gurney with no expression in my eyes.

With somebody looking over my limp form and trying to keep track of all the tubes.

And somebody else shaking his head and saying I'm a goner for sure this time.

I thought about the list of things I want to accomplish before I die.

The things I want to get out of life.

Two pages, easy.

And pedaled away with renewed resolve.

Fifteen men are in the suicide-watch cell this day at the old Vanderburgh County Jail. Prisoners are squeezed in so tight that someone sitting on the commode must pull his feet back to keep off another inmate's sleeping mat.

Guards take a head count every 15 minutes. Prisoners are allowed only a poncho and a blanket. No underwear. No belt. No shoes. The only reading matter is a Bible.

Inmates are closely supervised when allowed outside the cell to shave and shower. They can only be returned to general population when a mental health official gives approval. Due to the overcrowded conditions, it can take several days for an inmate to be evaluated.

Joe Sidener, 37, has been in the suicide cell for three months.

"Before, I was in the jail's third floor. If there's a hell on Earth, that's it. I got tired of watching men get beat up and being deprived of food.

"It wasn't because of anything that happened to me. I'm a pretty big guy. I can take care of myself. I just got tired of watching it happen to others. I told a female guard that I was having suicidal thoughts. That's true. I get them. But I had an ulterior motive. I wanted to get to a cell that I thought would be a better place."

Sidener is not so sure he made a good decision.

"At first, we had access to the commissary and everything was quiet. Then more and more guys came in the suicide cell and they took the commissary away. It's a tense atmosphere because we're worried about our cases. I saw one guy try to cut his wrist with a plastic spoon.

"If there's no room in isolation, they put those inmates in with us. One man was coming down off drugs and he went crazy. The guards used so much pepper spray on him that we had to leave the cell."

Sidener says he has spent almost half his life behind bars. As a younger man, he stole cars. More recently, he broke into businesses "and grabbed any cash that was sitting around."

He says he has post-traumatic stress disorder.

"It causes compulsive behavior. I'd have nightmares and wake up to panic attacks. The next thing I know, I'm driving around in my car and breaking into places."

Sometimes, Sidener says, he pilfered as much as $700. Equally often, he notes, the crime netted little or nothing.

"I never used a gun or any other weapon. Gaining entry was exciting. It was a stress-reliever to my compulsion."

He says the suicide cell shouldn't hold more than eight men.

"There's no privacy and you have to beg to get the room cleaned up. Some guards are nicer than others. You look for a little humanity, but it's few and far between."

Sidener says the men in the suicide cell "staged a little uprising" recently by keeping their food trays in the cell and by tying the door down.

"It's crowded, and when you don't get your shower on time, it's very stressful."

Joe Sidener has been sentenced to six years for burglary. He expects to leave the jail in a few days to start his term

"I'm done with my criminal life. The doctor says I can beat my condition with medication and talk therapy. I'm not a bad person. If you knew me, you'd like me. I'm not some low-life off the street."

I don't know what you did last night, but I had a track and field tournament.

Well, field.

I have a 16-pound shot put that I fling to keep fit, and in hope one of the neighbors will call the cops to report Paul Bunyan is loose.

My only competition was a kid from up the street whose heave could be measured in inches, and a ground squirrel that chose not to participate even after I offered to pay its entry fee.

Ah, winning. The good feeling never goes away.

I'll take your questions.

Isn't a shot put a strange toy for an adult?

Not really. I look at the thing as a marble that received too much human growth hormone. Its secret is safe with me, though. There will be no federal grand jury investigation in my back yard.

Is there a secret to flipping the shot put farther than a little neighbor kid?

Yes. You must have a good grunt, one that is uniquely your own. I favor "HARRUMGOOSBUH," but "PUCKAPUCKAWHOOSH" works just as well.

So that's why a shot-putter's face always looks like he's being Taser-ed?

Yes. You must have the proper swagger, the stiffer the legs the better. Our role model is Frankenstein's monster.

Do you practice safe shot put?

Not always. Some almost grown-ups who were on my kids' baseball teams years ago came over and we played catch with it. One fellow dropped the thing on his foot. We laughed hysterically. I can honestly say that's the highest level of guyness ever achieved on my property.

Is there some other reason to throw a heavy weight other than for the amusement of tiny male minds?

Yes. I do not own a gun. Prowlers to our abode will receive a face full of shot put. It should make for an interesting mug shot.

You sound anxious for this to happen.

I'm leaving the light on.

Is there any credence to the longstanding rumor that shot-putters lack intelligence?

I prefer to think we are sneaky smart. You buy expensive products to kill your grass. We throw the shot put. It is true, however, that we are shunned by proper society. There's something about grunting "HARRUMGOOSBUH" that keeps you from being invited to the home show.

Is there some sort of inner peace a shot-putter achieves after a good hurl?

I don't know about Zen, but the moles hate the round ball and that's good enough for me.

A grown man devaluing his property by throwing the shot put on his lawn. Sounds like a TV reality show.

I've got a can't-miss premise. Dangerous felons up for parole come to my back yard. If they beat me in the shot put, they're free men. Lose, and it's six more years of hard time. I call it, "Home or the Hole."

One last question. What's the best thing that can happen when throwing the shot put?

A moon landing.

Terry Blesch Was Happiest As Santa

ELBERFELD, Ind. – Terry Blesch was buried Monday afternoon. He died Friday of complications brought on by a lifelong struggle with asthma.

The 41-year-old Warrick County man drove a truck for a living, taking the wheel for the first time a few months after graduating high school. His last home office was in Iowa where he was dispatched on haul routes as far away as Texas and California.

Three weeks ago, maintenance workers found him slumped over the gearshift. It was several minutes before the rescue squad could get his heart started. The doctor told his parents, Edwin and Viola Blesch, it was only a matter of time until the end.

Terry was never one to get in a hurry and you couldn't make him mad. He knew the formula to turn strangers into friends.

He weighed 350 pounds, wore a thick beard and had a special love for children.

Perfect qualifications for a Santa Claus.

"He loved to get dressed up in that outfit," his father said at the funeral home. "Sometimes he'd get paid for it, but he didn't really care about the money. He really brightened up when there were kids around."

Edwin said his youngest son played Santa Claus more than 100 times. Private parties, company get-togethers, church functions – the smile was always the same.

"One time he left a hospital bed to be Santa. We tried to get him to stay in until he could breathe better, but he wouldn't hear of it. He had a little book that he kept his appointments in. If he told you he was coming, you could count on him."

Terry lived with his parents. He rarely dated and spent most of his off-road time at home.

"The only bad thing you could say about him was that he smoked too much," Edwin Blesch said. "He had one in his mouth a little before his heart stopped. 'This will be my last cigarette,' he told me. And it was. He knew the asthma was gonna get him one of these days. It was like he knew that time was coming."

The guy prided himself on being an authentic Santa. He dyed his beard white. He let children pat his belly. His "Ho, ho, ho" could be heard a block away.

Joanna Horne runs the Korner Inn, a tavern in Elberfeld. Terry Blesch was a regular customer.

"But only Pepsi," she said. "He didn't want the downtown children to smell anything on his breath."

She showed the pictures on the wall taken last Christmas when Terry made an impromptu visit in full Santa regalia.

"He had these candy canes and he passed them out to everybody in the bar. Customers took turns sitting in his lap. He made jokes about his weight, and said you can't be a decent Santa if you have to wear padding."

Edwin Blesh, 79, shook the hand of a family friend. Terry will be missed, she said. Truly happy people are hard to find.

The dad nodded.

"The children will know it most of all. Terry was already getting calls for Christmas. I guess they can find someone else to wear a Santa suit, but they can't do it the way Terry did."

October 15, 1992
Time For Luckless Man To Be Dealt New Cards

The thin man leaned against a guardrail on U.S. 41 south of Henderson, Ky., but kept his thumb in the hitchhiker's position. His cap was too big for his face. His baggy overalls clustered at his ankles. He looked tired.

I stopped. There was something about his face.

He told me his name is Bill Erwin. He said it was important that he get to Paducah, Ky., as soon as possible.

"My sister called last night and said Mom is getting worse. She had a stroke last month and now she's back in the hospital. The doctor thinks she might not make it. I've got to be there."

That corner of Western Kentucky wasn't where I was headed, but my plans were easy enough to change.

My passenger said he is 58 years old, but he looks older. He said he is down to his last $2, and that he had been homeless until a few months ago when he started staying at a shelter in Henderson. He said he has no bank account and gets no money from the government.

I explained that I work for the newspaper and asked if he wanted to talk.

"I've got nothing to hide," the toothless man replied.

Erwin said he grew up in Evansville, the son of a railroad worker, and that he started "nipping from the bottle" when he was in high school. He said he hopped his first freight train at age 9.

"After I graduated, I hoboed whenever I felt like it. I never wanted to get settled down."

He said he used to drink as much as two fifths of wine a day. A year ago, a bleeding ulcer forced him to seek medical attention. The doctor told him another bout with the bottle could kill him.

"I haven't had a taste since then. I go to church twice a week and AA meetings three times a week. When my old drinking buddies come around, I tell 'em I'm not interested."

Erwin said he has had "40 or more" different jobs, but that he never stayed at one place longer than 18 months. He said he worked at several furniture factories in the Evansville area, "but then I'd get on a drunk and they'd lay me off." He said one sympathetic boss appreciated his skill and kept a pint of whiskey handy "so I wouldn't get the DTs."

He told me he never made more than $5.80 an hour. His preferred way of payment was cash at the end of the day "so I'd have some folding money in case I took a notion to leave. I can say one thing. I've had a lot of adventures."

Being a ranch hand in Wyoming. Picking fruit in California. Digging holes for septic tanks in upstate Illinois.

"But wherever I was, I always stayed in contact with my mother. She's the most important person in my life."

He said he rarely hopped a train when sober. Once he was so drunk that he woke up in St. Louis and couldn't remember how he got there.

"I don't blame anybody else for my problems. I was dealt a tough hand, but I didn't help myself any."

Erwin said he had been hitchhiking about an hour before I picked him up. He said he picks up aluminum cans, but couldn't find enough to pay for a bus ticket.

"I'm a hard worker – painting, being a janitor, staying with old folks, whatever. People don't want to hire me because they think I'm still drinking. But I'm gonna straighten myself out. I'm a better person now. When I was young, I was restless all the time. Now I just want to stay home."

He said he rinses his gums in saltwater so it doesn't hurt so much when he eats meat. He said he sometimes rummages through the trash for bread and pies.

"It's been rough, that's for sure."

I took my passenger to the front door of Lourdes Hospital in Paducah. He waved goodbye and walked inside. I never saw him again. I hope he was dealt some better cards.

HENDERSON, Ky. – Oswald "Poss" Coomes has been arrested for possession of illegal slot machines and dice games. He's peddled home brew. He's sold monkeys.

The 89-year-old man has been arrested for stocking illegal fireworks. He's been buddies to bootleggers. He's "drank too much and chased after too many women."

The former tavern owner battled polio, and "went through more money than you could believe. You could say that when I look back at my life, it takes a pretty long time."

Coomes operated the Kentucky Tavern in the late 1940s when Henderson was teeming with beer halls and whiskey joints.

"You couldn't make any money running just a place to eat and drink. If you didn't do something that was illegal, it was bad business."

So Coomes – like many of the other tavern operators – had slots and dice.

"Everybody was paid off, so you didn't have to worry about being busted. My slots went from a nickel to a silver dollar. The payout was about 85 percent. If you set the things too tight, people wouldn't play 'em."

The end came in 1951, Coomes recalls, when the Good Government League came into being and put pressure on law enforcement to crack down on the backroom games at the taverns.

"I think they indicted something like 42 different people, me included. We had all the lawyers in town defending us, so it was a whole bunch against the prosecuting attorney. Nobody ended up serving any time. I don't remember how much my fine was, but it wasn't much. They took my machines, though."

He talks about growing up in rural McLean County, Ky., and getting his nickname as a toddler "when all the old women thought I was cuter than a possum."

And about going to a Louisville hospital for successful polio treatment.

Garret Mathews   157

"I took that shoe brace off when I was 7 and set it aside for 80 years until my foot started acting up, and I had to wear the same kind of brace. What kind of thing is that?"

He talks about being married "11 different times. Why? Because I was crazy. I should've stayed with the first one."

At age 12, Poss met a bootlegger who introduced the boy to the concept of "blinds" -- places that seemed to be restaurants, but were really fronts for illegal hooch.

"I've always been able to make connections. I'll bet I know more than a thousand people by their first names. Back when I kept getting busted, they'd drag me in front of a six-person jury. I'd always have at least one buddy in the bunch and sometimes two or three. That's why the law couldn't do much with me."

Poss said the tavern owners met every Monday night at the Club Trocadero near the Kentucky-Indiana line.

"That was to sort things out, to make sure everybody knew what was going on. One time we heard these mob guys from St. Louis were gonna offer us three times more for our places than they were worth. We got told not to sell because this was the kind of crowd that would hire somebody to kill you if you crossed 'em. We all held firm and they went back where they came from."

Poss heard a lot of sob stories and believed some.

"A woman would come in and say her husband lost his entire paycheck to the slots and dice at my joint. We always had a policy to give the money back if we thought the person was sincere. It was cheaper than having them take out warrants on you all the time."

After selling the Kentucky Tavern, he opened the Red Horse Gift Shop in Henderson.

"I would change some of my habits if I could do it all over, but I wouldn't change the way I made a living. I love people. The jobs I had put me with all kinds."

It's my day to spend time with a couple of elementary schoolchildren I know from the poor side of the city.

We're off to the lake on the East Side of town to watch a bunch of radio-controlled miniature boats take hot laps.

A little girl from across the street runs toward the van.

"Mister, can I go where my friends are going? Please! I don't get many extra trips and I won't be any trouble."

Her father is in the back yard. I ask if he's OK with his daughter tagging along.

The guy shrugs his shoulders. Clearly, he has other things on his mind than where his child will be spending the next few hours.

He doesn't kiss her goodbye. He doesn't even look back.

She doesn't act surprised.

The little girl is delightful company. She's well-mannered and likes to laugh.

The kids are only somewhat interested in watching a bunch of toy boats go vroom-vroom. Cups in hand, they wade in a few feet and try to catch some baby fish.

I overhear them talking about not having an aquarium at home, but maybe they can get a glass bowl at the Dollar Store.

This is hardly news. A lot of children in this part of Evansville live in grinding poverty. One child of my acquaintance stays in a downstairs living space carved out next to the furnace. It's filthy. Another has a tiny apartment with holes in the porch and whack marks on the door.

I overhear my two regular kids tell the new girl that we occasionally stop at a restaurant for a snack. The new girl says she's sure she's been to a restaurant some time in her life, but can't remember when.

I pull in for ice cream. She asks how many scoops she can have. "All you want," I reply. She asks for one. "I don't want to be greedy."

When we get back to the neighborhood, I offer to walk the new girl across the street.

She tells me not to bother, that her father probably has forgotten that she was even gone.

Flash forward a few weeks. I'm back to take my two regular kids on another outing.

"Did you hear what happened?" they ask.

No, what?

"Do you remember the new girl who went with us to the little boats?"

Yes. Is she sick or something?

"Not sick. Gone."

They explain that the dad was arrested for making meth. The new girl was taken to Child Protective Services.

The sun went behind a cloud. That fit my mood.

The new girl had gotten an extra trip all right, but not a good one. And, I feared, not her last.

For This Old Soldier, The War Isn't Over

A man calls. He is crying.

"There's something I have to know before I die. I'm 81 years old. Who am I kidding? There isn't much time. You're the guy who's written a lot about Second World War veterans, right?"

Yes.

"I've never told anybody this before because I know I can't get through it. Can you understand?"

I think so.

"Do you think you can help me find someone before it's too late?"

I'll try.

"It's not someone. He's gone. It's his family I want to get hold of."

The person on the other end of the line apologizes for being emotional. Then he blurts it out.

"I killed a man."

The crying gets louder.

"I need to make it right before I die. I want to talk, but I don't want to talk. Can you understand?"

I think so.

"It was in France or Germany. I can't remember any more. It was the winter after D-Day. We had taken this hill that looked like one of the Pennsylvania mountains and we were dug in foxholes to defend it. Two- and three-man trenches. The perimeter was set up in circles that went all the way around the mountain. We were holed in about 30 feet apart.

"Snow was up to our butts. We were very edgy. We knew the enemy was coming up the hill. They were in white snowsuits to make it harder for us to pick them out. They even had their rifles wrapped.

"The orders were to stay in our holes. With visibility the way it was, anything out of the hole would be considered the enemy. Time passed and we heard sniper rounds. Grenades were going off, too. We knew some of our holes had been infiltrated.

"When they said not to leave the hole, they meant not to leave the hole. For any reason. If you had to go to the bathroom, you went in your steel helmet. When you got a chance, you threw the waste out the side.

"I found out later that this kid – this 18-year-old from Tennessee – had to relieve himself. He was on angle left from our position. He climbed out of the foxhole and stood next to a tree."

My caller starts crying again.

"I couldn't help it. We were scared. Can you understand? He was a shadow. I thought he was one of them. So I squeezed off a round with my M1. I heard a thud in the darkness.

"The next morning, we looked around for casualties. I looked on the angle left. There he was. Gone."

The receiver goes dead for a few seconds.

"It's been more than 55 years. It was war, right? You're supposed to forget."

More crying.

"I can't."

The Evansville man wants to contact members of the soldier's family. He wants to explain how the young man died. And to say he's sorry.

"I'll travel to wherever he lives. We can throw our arms around each other. I want them to see me and I want to see them. I'd like to have some peace in the time I have left."

He doesn't have the man's first or last name, but knows his unit and his age.

Maybe someone will read this who knows about war records and databases.

And induce a machine to spit out the information.

Which I'll pass along.

Before it's too late.

No one came forward with any information. The elderly man never called again.

WINSLOW, Ind. – Bill Johnson, 79, lives in a group home in this Pike County town with six other adults who have mental and physical shortcomings.

With staff supervision, they prepare meals, do their own laundry and clean their rooms.

Not much is known about Bill's past, other than he grew up on a farm not far from Fort Wayne, Ind., and spent many years in an orphanage.

"My mother, she might still be alive. I don't know. I wish I could see her."

Talking about his family makes him sad. So Bill changes the subject.

"I love animals. When I was little, I had rabbits. Lots of rabbits."

He walks Ollie, the big mixed-breed dog that lives on the premises. He also feeds the several cats, some of which he brought to the facility.

"I walk in the woods and find them. It's easy. It's like they stop for me."

Twice a week, Bill volunteers at the animal shelter in nearby Petersburg. He scrubs kennels and makes sure every dog gets a treat.

"I play with the new kittens and the new puppies. It's my best day of all."

Paul Brewster, a former lawman, is a staff member at the group home.

"Bill's been with us almost 20 years, longer than anybody. He's usually very happy. Very seldom is he sad."

Brewster says Bill has told stories about running away from the orphanage and drinking and getting in trouble.

"For too many years, the system wasn't set up for people like Bill. They don't belong in jail and they don't belong in a mental institution. A place like we have is a go-between."

Bill pets a cat with a limp that came from the woods.

"We're his only family," Brewster says.

Bill shows me his room. There are posters, pictures and statuettes of animals. There are videotapes of movies about animals.

"This is my guinea pig," he says proudly, sticking a finger in the cage.

The animal is huge. There are several buckets of feed in the room. It's possible that Bill overdoes it.

"And these are my goldfish. You can't put two in the same bowl because they'll fight."

He opens a box and takes out a brightly colored outfit.

"This was my Halloween costume. I want to get a new one for next year."

Bill talks about going to Princeton, Ind., with other residents of the group home where they work putting handles on buckets.

"We get money. We go to the bank on Thursdays. Sometimes I save."

Bill had a heart attack last fall. Staff members make sure he remembers to take his medicine. They tag along when he walks in the woods looking for stray cats.

"I like doing the buckets," Bill says, "but I like being with the animals more. Tomorrow is the day I get to go see them. I'll have a glad face the whole time."

Stephen Ralph runs his fingers over the strings of the Fender Stratocaster.

"This feels really good. It's been a long time."

The 37-year-old native of California is homeless. He has no place to store the guitar, so it's in safekeeping at a pawnshop.

Ralph had nothing better to do on this cold afternoon, so he visits his instrument.

"Some people ask me, 'Hey, maybe you could get a couple thousand bucks for it and get back on your feet.' I shake my head to that. I play music. The guitar is part of who I am."

He says he had a double major in English and music at San Bernardino Valley College. His favorite courses were guitar theory and music composition.

"I played in some bands. Had some fun. But that's a long way in the past."

It's lunchtime at the United Caring Shelter in Evansville. Several dozen men and women dig into their helpings of spaghetti.

Some are just here for the meal. Ralph is one of 62 men who spend the night. He's been a resident almost six months.

"I was a pharmacy technician in Los Angeles. I wrote songs for commercials. I had a good life."

Then his mother died.

"We were very close. She had leukemia and was slowly slipping away. When I wasn't working, I was caring for her. I took her passing badly. I couldn't deal with it."

Ralph says his drinking intensified until he was consuming a half-gallon of gin a day.

"Because of the alcohol, I made a lot of questionable decisions. Everything escalated in a negative direction."

He says he took a bus from Los Angeles to Kansas City where he spent three months at a rescue mission. Then he went to Nashville, Tenn., and lived six weeks in a shelter before coming to Evansville.

"I went through the 12-day program at Stepping Stone. I had the DTs and couldn't sleep and was pretty much a wreck, but the treatment worked. I haven't had a drink since the summer."

Ralph finishes the last of his salad.

"I'm a spiritual man. I go to chapel. I believe in my heart that 2009 will be a better time for me."

Other than the guitar, he has few possessions other than clothes. He earns $50 a week selling plasma, "but right now I'm pretty much broke."

Ralph spends most days at the library, where he uses the computer to put in job applications. He also walks through the book aisles.

"Reading is free," he says, grinning.

Tightening his black overcoat, Ralph looks around the cafeteria at the shelter.

"There are lots of people in this room who held jobs in different fields – welding, roofing, whatever – and now there's nothing for them. I could just as easy be homeless because of the tough economy instead of alcohol."

He says he tries to keep a positive attitude.

"If you live in a place like this with no hope, it's easy to give up. If I have a poor mindset, how can I expect anything to change? Regardless of how devastated you feel, you have to hold your head up."

Stephen Ralph says he has 12 years in the pharmacy industry.

"I have a world of experience. But facts are facts. If you put down a homeless shelter as a residence, that's a big strike against your job search."

The goal, he says, is to return to California when he can afford the $200 for a bus ticket.

"But since I'm in Evansville, why not pull myself up right here? At least I don't have to worry about where I'll sleep every night."

I want to tell you about something that led the league in personal humiliation when I was in high school.

Nothing else came close to making a 15-year-old male – his face a bright crimson – want his family to take the night train to Burma.

I'm talking about the rope you had to climb to pass the physical fitness test.

Knotted on the end, it dangled from the top girder of the gymnasium.

The PE teacher said it was only 40 feet high, but it was at least a mile.

Mortification could come in many ways.

You could fall, hit your head on the floor and spend the rest of your life in the trauma ward.

You could lack the strength to make it to the top. The PE teacher – always eager to bring another weakling out of the closet – would have the news all over the school by lunch. People you don't even know will ask if you need help lifting your peas.

Or you could freeze up, lock your hands in a vice grip around the rope and vow never to move. The subsequent emergency call to the psychiatrist would keep you from ever being popular.

I had a fear of heights. Why couldn't they dig a hole in the floor and have us climb down?

But it was being singled out that I dreaded the most.

To my young brain, all other activity at the school stopped during my appointment with the rope.

There was no cooking in home economics. No dissecting in biology. No passing notes in study hall.

Enquiring minds – hundreds of them – were peering through the windows of the gymnasium, each equipped with high-powered transmitters to relay the news to listening posts at other schools across the nation.

"Next, Heslep," the PE teacher barked.

Like a dead boy walking, Steve makes his way front and center.

Will he get to the girder?

Or languish on the knot?

Steve has the upper-body strength of a dead sparrow and advances maybe two feet.

"Next, Powers."

Roger would later laugh at the SAT test because it was so easy. He would later teach at the University of Notre Dame.

But he couldn't get to the top of the rope if he had a missile launcher in his butt.

"Next, Mathews."

I would rather sing the national anthem at Yankee Stadium without benefit of vocal cords.

I push off the knot. Slowly, inches at a time, I make my way to the top of the building.

Charlie got up and down in 15 seconds; J.D. in 25.

Mine would be a climb across the sands of time.

A minute passes. The girder is two body lengths away. I summon my sinews to go once more into the breach.

Please, Lord, I'll be an acolyte for the rest of my life. Just don't let me fail.

I got up. I got down.

Time: 1 minute, 50 seconds. The slowest in the class, and if you believe the gym teacher, the slowest of any pissant kid in the Free World.

But I passed the fitness test.

How did I celebrate?

Lifted everybody's peas at lunch.

Charles Carter, 78, died last Thursday.

There were no immediate survivors.

He was buried Monday afternoon at Oak Hill Cemetery in Evansville.

No one came.

Two men from the funeral home set up the blue tent and put six chairs beside the gravesite.

They don't know Mr. Carter or anyone who does, but maybe an old buddy or two read the obituary in the newspaper.

The men wait five minutes after the scheduled 1:30 burial.

Just in case the mourners got caught up in traffic.

Or couldn't find the plot in the sprawling cemetery.

But no one came.

The men from the funeral home say a few prayers from the minister's book they keep in the hearse.

The workman from the vault company bows his head.

And then puts his gloves on, grabs the rope and begins the slow process of lowering the casket into the ground.

The coroner signed the death certificate and the bank verified Mr. Carter's Social Security number so it could be taken off the books.

Standard procedure.

But no one claimed the body.

Not standard.

The coroner called the funeral home.

It would be a pauper's burial. No visitation. No minister. No headstone.

One of the morticians took clothes from his closet so Mr. Carter could be properly attired.

"This happens more often than people think," one man from the funeral home says.

"Sad. Very sad," his colleague says. "To go out alone."

It's 1:40 p.m. The men from the funeral home decide to wait a little longer.

Just in case.

A hearse enters the front gate of the cemetery. More than a dozen cars follow. The procession winds around the road in sight of Mr. Carter's plot. Younger men and women help the elderly to their seats under the tent. Every chair is filled.

It's 1:45 p.m.

The workman from the vault company has the casket almost in place. Just a few more tugs on the ropes.

The men from the funeral home says cremation was considered.

"But we didn't go that route because maybe some day someone will want to stop by and pay respects," one explains. "The burial provides a piece of ground for them to look at."

The workman is finished. He folds his green rug and gathers his boards.

It's 1:50 p.m.

The men from the funeral home look one last time to see if any latecomers are making their way to the pauper's plot.

Nobody.

A call comes in on the cell phone.

"We're clear," one replies. "Nothing going on here."

They drive away.

I look at the grave.

No flowers.

No reminders of a life lived.

Just a half-filled pop bottle on an adjoining stone.

And a pile of smoothed-over dirt.

No one came.

For a book project a few years ago that never got off the ground, I collected oral histories from about 50 men and women who were active in the civil rights movement in the 1950s and '60s.

I talked with some folks who participated in sit-ins at lunch counters and others who went to the South to register black voters. They faced massive resistance from the white establishment. Some were beaten. Almost all were threatened.

Hank Thomas was a 19-year-old college student when he joined the Freedom Riders in 1961. Volunteers boarded buses and headed to Mississippi and Alabama to draw attention to the continued segregation at interstate transportation facilities that was in violation of federal law.

The idea was for white riders to attempt to buy tickets at the black-only counter, and African-Americans to do the same at the white-only facility.

The civil rights workers expected to be arrested. On one bus, they were almost killed.

This is Thomas' story.

"I had been involved with lunch counter sit-ins in Maryland and Virginia. Never had any mustard thrown on me, though. I'm a pretty big fellow, and if you're a young coward, you'll pick on somebody else other than me.

"The further south we went, the worse it got. In Winnsboro, (S.C.), the police took me out of jail in the middle of the night and delivered me to this mob that had formed at the bus station. I thought I was going to be killed. Fortunately, a brave black man in town was watching the police and reported what he saw to federal authorities.

"That was a close call, but it made me more determined to keep going. Throughout history, people who are oppressed have taken risks to change their situation. Some lost their lives. That's just how it goes.

"Then the bus moved on to Anniston (Ala.). We were told this would be rough. They weren't lying. The streets were deserted. Everybody was at the bus station. All male. All white. All screaming.

"They beat on the bus and slashed the tires. We didn't get very far out of town when the tires went flat. Outside was another mob. Well-dressed, Christian, white people who had brought their children to witness lynchings.

"Some kind of incendiary device was thrown into the bus. If I got off the bus, I would be beaten to death. If I stayed, the fire would get me. I thought the easiest way to die would be to remain on the bus. It would be like breathing too much ether. You just close your eyes and go to sleep.

"The smoke got real bad, and we were vomiting. I staggered off the bus and a man hit me in the head with a baseball bat. A state trooper was standing next to him and didn't say a word.

"We needed to go to the hospital, but it wasn't that easy. At that time, a white-owned ambulance company couldn't transport African-Americans. We had to wait by the side of the road, bleeding, for the black-owned ambulance.

"It took a long time for the bitterness inside me to go away. It was so wrong. I held what happened inside for years and years.

"I was a medic in Vietnam, and this white Southerner got shot up pretty bad. I treated him, and he threw his arms around me and thanked me for saving his life.

"I couldn't help but think, yeah, well, I did all that, but what would you have done if you saw me on that bus in Anniston?"

PORTERSVILLE, Ind. – Sept. 16, 1959. Cleo Fisher's truck is hit head-on by another semi-trailer a few miles outside Chicago. He is paralyzed below the shoulders. His only recollection is pulling out of the parking lot on the morning of the collision.

"They operated on me, and the doctors said I would eventually regain the use of my legs," recalls the Dubois County man, now 81. "I kept pulling my chest hair out and eagerly waiting for the day when I could feel something. After about six months, I knew it wasn't gonna happen. I never blamed the doctors, 'cause they tell everybody the same thing to give you hope so you won't wanna kill yourself."

It's been almost 50 years since the accident and the resulting 12 months in hospitals "when all I could do was shake my head. My hands and fingers eventually worked out OK, but that's it."

But Cleo Fisher's mood is upbeat. He laughs frequently and cusses comfortably.

"I know that most people who have my kind of accident are lucky to live 20 years, much less as long as I have. I'm glad to have hands and fingers that can do something. God's been good."

He looks at shelves piled full of small appliances, toasters, shavers and coffee makers. There is absolutely no organizational scheme.

"Being bored is the worst that can happen when you're like me. I don't thank customers for the money they give me. I thank them for the work."

Fisher's Home Appliances Repair has been in business since the early 1970s. The proprietor jokes that getting something fixed at his place is about the only reason to drive to the unincorporated community a few miles north of Jasper.

"This is a graveyard for parts and products. I guess you could say we're a little old-fashioned."

The shop is a cinderblock building that used to be a motel. Inside are a few new vacuum cleaners, but there are many, many more ancient ones in various stages of repair.

"About 800 in all," Fisher estimates.

Figure to spend $8.50 if your electric shaver is on the fritz. Sewing machine repairs are around $34.95. He'll ring up the sale on a 1940 cash register.

The man served in the Second World War and later got in the trucking business. He owned five dump trucks before taking on the semi-trailer job driving to and from Chicago.

After the accident, he spent most of his time fishing and hunting squirrel.

"I rigged up a tractor so I could get to where I was going and back. But I got tired of that real fast. I knew I had to find something to do or I'd go crazy. I had a bunch of old tools and stuff in the house. I moved 'em to the old motel I had rebuilt and figured I'd try making repairs."

Several stores in and around Jasper send their fix-it business his way. He also gets plenty of word-of-mouth backing from folks who figured there was no way their Bunn Coffee Maker would ever brew another cup, only to find out Fisher got the thing percolating good as new.

Bacteria is building up in his right foot. Doctors say they might have to amputate. The ace repairman doesn't much care.

"I already can't feel anything down there. Won't make a whole lot of difference if I can't see anything down there either."

Some people want to know why an 81-year-old man is still poring over shaving heads.

"Let's say I don't get up at 5 a.m. like I'm supposed to so I can make it to the shop on time. Let's say I get up at 6. And the next day it's 7. Pretty soon I'd be spending all my time in bed. No way for that."